Test Less Assess More

A K-8 Guide to Formative Assessment

Leighangela Brady and Lisa McColl

EYE ON EDUCATION
6 DEPOT WAY WEST, SUITE 106
LARCHMONT, NY 10538
(914) 833–0551
(914) 833–0761 fax
www.eyeoneducation.com

Library of Congress Cataloging-in-Publication Data

Brady, Leighangela.

  Test less, assess more : a K-8 guide to formative assessment / Leighangela Brady and Lisa Mc-Coll.

      p. cm.

  Includes bibliographical references.

  ISBN 978-1-59667-130-0

  1. Education, Elementary—United States—Evaluation. 2. Educational tests and measure-ments. 3. Academic achievement—United States. I. McColl, Lisa.

  II. Title.

  LA219.B73 2010

  372.126'4—dc22

                                                                              2009025113

10 9 8 7 6 5 4 3 2 1

Also Available from EYE ON EDUCATION

Formative Assessment:
Responding to Your Students
Harry Grover Tuttle

Math Intervention:
Building Number Power with Formative
Assessments, Differentiation and Games
Jennifer Taylor-Cox

Teacher-Made Assessments:
Connecting Curriculum, Instruction, and Student Learning
Christopher R. Gareis and Leslie W. Grant

Data, Data Everywhere:
Bringing All the Data Together for
Continuous School Improvement
Victoria L. Bernhardt

Short Cycle Assessment:
Improving Student Achievement
Through Formative Assessment
Susan Lang, Todd Stanley, and Betsy Moore

Differentiated Assessment for
Middle and High School Classrooms
Deborah Blaz

Differentiating Assessment in
Middle and High School English and Social Studies
Sheryn Spencer Waterman

Differentiating Assessment in
Middle and High School Mathematics and Science
Sheryn Spencer Waterman

Formative Assessment for English Language Arts:
A Guide for Middle and High School Teachers
Amy Benjamin

Differentiating by Student Interest:
Strategies and Lesson Plans
Joni Turville

Meet the Authors

Born and raised in New England, **Leighangela Brady** received both her B.S. and M.A. degrees from the University of Connecticut. Now living in San Diego, Mrs. Brady has taught in various teaching assignments from kindergarten through fifth grade, including a bilingual placement and specialized pullout instruction for English Learners. After leaving the classroom, Leighangela became an academic literacy coach for teachers. This position ignited an already sparked passion for curriculum and instruction and helped to further develop her strength as a curriculum leader. Within a few years, Leighangela became a vice principal in a unique K-8 setting. She is currently serving as a principal of a K-6 elementary school. As a site administrator, educational consultant, and instructional leader, Mrs. Brady is passionate about quality teaching. She is a wife and mother as well as cofounder of a small company called *Teaching Simply*. Leighangela plans to retire one day to her home in the Fiji Islands.

As a California native, **Lisa McColl** received both her B.S. and M.A. degrees from San Diego State University. Mrs. McColl has taught in various settings including both private and public schools and has worked with a variety of students from kindergarten through eighth grade including students identified as Gifted and Talented. After leaving the classroom, Lisa became a Language Arts demonstration teacher/instructional coach and was fortunate to be able to share her passion for advancing all levels of learning with teachers at multiple grade levels and on multiple sites. Lisa soon moved into the position of site administration and has been active as an instructional leader for the past 9 years. Her commitment to life-long learning has guided her career path. She is currently serving as a principal of a K-8 elementary school as well as teaching at Chapman University. As cofounder of a small company called *Teaching Simply*, Lisa continues her work in order to ensure that all students achieve maximum levels of success.

Contents

Free Downloads

The tools and forms in the Appendix are also available on Eye On Education's web site: www.eyeoneducation.com. Book buyers have been granted permission to print out these Adobe Acrobat© documents and duplicate them to distribute to your students.

You can access these downloads by visiting Eye On Education's website: www. eyeoneducation.com. Click on FREE Downloads or search or browse our website to find this book and then scroll down for downloading instructions. You'll need your book-buyer access code: **TBM-7130–0**

Foreword

Imagine that you've been looking forward to your ideal vacation. Your bags are packed and you have a full tank of gas in the car. The vacation time has been approved and you're on the road. Although you have a general idea of where you are headed, you don't have a specific destination or the road map to get there. Without the end in mind, how will you know when you've arrived?

Teachers often find themselves in a similar scenario in their classrooms. It's not uncommon to watch a teacher working really hard and spending countless hours trying to make a difference in the achievement levels of the students. They know the standards, they use strong instructional strategies, and yet they just don't know if the students are mastering the concepts being taught. Stephen Covey, in his book *7 Habits of Highly Effective People* (1989), tells us, "To begin with the end in mind means to start with a clear understanding of your destination. It means to know where you are going so that you better understand where you are now so that the steps you take are always in the right direction" (pp. 95–96). Without a road map (curriculum map, pacing guide), planned stops along the way (formative assessments, student work samples, and teacher observations), and a final destination (grade level benchmarks, summative assessments, state standards), teachers will continue to spin their wheels in the sand.

Likewise, without a predetermined destination in mind and proper means to get there, administrators may find that they are leading the flock astray. Site- or district-level superintendents, directors, coordinators, principals, assistant principals, support staff, and coaches must all be working toward the same goals. Each member of the team must understand his or her role and be able to support the teachers who are on the front line. Support roles are essential in helping to set and maintain our course and to be able to effectively intervene when bumps arise or breakdowns occur.

The first step of the journey is identifying the target. It is essential that there be a written set of curriculum goals, standards, and objectives for all teachers to teach and a commitment from all teachers to teach it. To provide equity of education for all students, all students must have access to the same curriculum objectives. A written curriculum does not eliminate teachers' instructional creativity, but provides teacher accountability for student learning. This written curriculum must be tightly held at the district level and consistently taught in all classrooms.

Administrators play a critical role in ensuring this consistency. Establishing cohesive teams that work together is imperative. Teachers should visibly see that expectations have been set, and that their hard work is both recognized and valued. This can be easily achieved through constant monitoring and timely feedback. Administrators have to be skilled at identifying the strengths and needs of teachers and be able to act as a coach in extending those skills to the next level. Teachers must have access to ongoing professional development and collaboration opportunities to fuel their efforts. Administrators, who are skillfully navigating, consistently fulfill these needs.

When we as educators know exactly what the students need to know and be able to do, we can provide a logical sequence of learning with connectors, not gaps, across the grade levels. We can also coordinate the curriculum within a grade level so as to ensure that all students have access to the same learning. This emphasizes the necessity of identifying essential standards for all subject matters, in all grade levels, and articulation throughout.

Once there is a written curriculum, it must be aligned to the taught and tested curriculum. If these areas are not aligned, teachers may as well be turning in circles. Formative assessments given along the way will guide the instruction and help to monitor the alignment of this instruction. The summative assessments used at the end of the course will continue to provide us with general information about our overall progress. Although the curriculum used should be tightly held, aligned to standards, and taught consistently in every classroom, the instructional methods are still a teacher's decision based on students' needs.

William Glasser, in his book *The Quality School Teacher*, urges us that the only way education is going to change is if the classroom teacher makes it happen. Consider any job in any field. Professionals notably know how to do the job they are hired to do, and they are most likely given an opportunity to do that job the way they believe is best. This is quite different than the way most schools are run. Traditionally, teachers are handed required textbooks and then given a message to teach the curriculum with fidelity. Teachers more often than not, interpret this as having to teach the "textbook" as the intended curriculum. Alas, if textbooks alone could guarantee student success, then we wouldn't need teachers, and we wouldn't be writing this book.

Consequently, to maximize achievement for students, we need to ensure that teachers are also given the tools to identify the essential standards and key learnings necessary for student success. Furthermore, they need support and trust to decide the best means of instruction to meet the curricular goals. When this happens, teachers no longer find themselves moving from page to page and unit to unit without being able to articulate the specific learning objectives. Instead, they are empowered to use those objectives to differentiate their instruction for each student thus creating a cycle of continuous improvement and refinement.

Administrators should be encouraged to provide teachers with this professional discretion. They ought to appreciate that it is the people who build the programs and hence focus their efforts on building capacity among their staff. However, that is not to say that teachers using poor instructional or assessment methods should be allowed to continue. It is the administrator who is responsible to make certain that teachers are choosing and using methods supported by current research. By the same token, administrators often need to act as a coach to influence some teachers to give up an outdated focus on a beloved topic (such as "the bear unit") in favor of a focus on curriculum goals and objectives.

After learning objectives have been identified, the next step is to identify the purpose and benefits behind the many different assessment tools that constantly bombard teachers. Do we have a clear understanding of the appropriate time and place for each assessment given or do we continue to fall into the pattern of giving the test at the end of the chapter because that is what the textbook publishers have given us? How do we determine the need for summative versus formative tests? Are we able to clearly articulate the difference between the two?

In this book you will learn ways to refine your practice as an elementary school educator by delving deep into the assessments we use with students in the classroom. We are going to take a critical look at how we use testing, so that we can move from a system of testing, testing, testing, to a more practical use of true assessment. This system will provide practical ways for teachers to gather data on what students know and are able to do to better instruct them in their next steps of learning. Administrators will be better skilled at supporting these efforts and be able to refine the systems imposed on teachers. You will see how these strategies help to identify the areas that students need to focus on to master the key concepts and standards or extend their learning in any given area. By "reducing the layers" we will help teachers "find time" in the day to differentiate instruction to ensure success for all students.

More often than not, we hear teachers express the frustration that they believe they are constantly giving students test after test, leaving no time to follow up with the instructional piece. We propose a shift in thinking. How can we collect that same data of student learning without putting another test in front of students? To do this, we must clearly define the roles of testing and assessment and realize that they are not the same thing. A test can be an instrument we use for assessment, but not all assessment comes in the form of a test. Again, this will entail administrators committing to allowing teachers professional discretion.

In addition to deciding how we are going to assess students, we will also need to understand how to use the data from those assessments to make instructional decisions. We will need to know how to collect and record that data so that this process can become a cyclical pattern of continual assessment; not just "It's the end of the term so I need to average up your grades to report your achievement." When administrators see a pattern such as this, a key question should be, "What purpose do assessments serve?" If the answer is only to collect grades for a report card, then the work must begin at the ground level. We must change how we view and use assessments before they can become the valuable information tool for which they were designed.

We have heard for more than a decade that this paradigm shift needs to occur. So why do we still see the same traditional pattern of testing in classrooms? The answer is simple: We haven't been told how to make the shift! Many researchers and resources provide information that spark thinking and raise awareness for what we need to do and why we need to do it. In the absence of a laid-out system in which to tackle this complex approach to assessment, we resort to a comfortable, manageable format.

Our hope is to provide insight into the "how." To offer practical, simple ideas and strategies that enable educators to take that next step toward implementation. However, we need to caution you that although these solutions may be simple, the work involved is not easy. It necessitates looking honestly into our systems and perhaps giving up traditional and already established norms. It means changing the way we do business and the way we expect business to be done. It entails reexamining our map and recharting our course to find the best possible route.

This book provides examples that span multiple grade levels, from kindergarten through eighth grade; however, the same principles can and should be applied in advanced levels of learning. Likewise, the concepts outlined are not intended to be used in isolation with one particular group of students or within one particular content area. Thus, these approaches can be applied to the unique demands of topics such as *Response to Intervention,* as well as to targeted groups such as English learners. They are meant as tools and strategies to be added to a toolbox of already successful approaches we utilize in our daily trade.

Whether you are a teacher, a site administrator, or in upper-level support, this book offers you insight in how to move toward a more productive approach to collecting data and monitoring student progress. It takes you on a journey of discovery and leaves you with new perspectives: determine the true purpose of assessment in chapter 1, explore reasons for the gap between data analysis and action in chapter 2, then streamline the assessment process in chapters 3 through 6 by identifying learning objectives, collecting data, recording evidence, and refining instruction. The result will be a greater positive impact on student achievement and an arrival at your ultimate destination!

1

So Many Tests—
What's the Purpose?

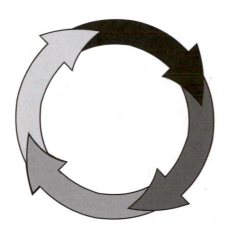

A shift of thinking regarding testing and assessment raises essential questions for educators. How do we know that students are learning what we are teaching them, and if they are not, what is our next step? DuFour, Eaker, and DuFour (2005) clearly state their premise that "students will be better served if educators embraced learning rather than teaching as the mission of their school" (p. 5). For those ready to embark on such a shift in thinking, we suggest taking a moment to first clearly define the jargon of testing and assessment. Too often we use words synonymously that have very different definitions. Take a minute and quiz yourself to see how clear you are on the key terms listed in Figure 1.1.

Figure 1.1. Pop Quiz: How Well Do You Know Testing and Assessment Jargon?

Match each term with its definition

1. Assessment	A. A type of assessment consisting of a set of questions administered at a given point in time.
2. Test	B. A test that reports results according to how others in the group perform.
3. Formative Assessment	C. A form of performance assessment structured around a real-life problem or situation.
4. Summative Assessment	D. A full range of procedures used to gain information about student learning and the formation of value judgments concerning student learning.
5. Norm-Referenced Test	E. A type of assessment usually occurring at the end of instruction or unit used to measure extent to which skills have been mastered.
6. Criterion-Referenced Test	F. A test designed to measure performance of a clearly defined learning goal.
7. Authentic Assessment	G. Assessment occurring during the learning process that provides ongoing information regarding student progress.

Answers: 1. D, 2. A, 3. G, 4. E, 5. B, 6. F, 7. C

Even with the nonthreatening pop-quiz format of matching answers, one can begin to see how easily the waters become muddied when trying to define assessment. A test can be a type of assessment, but every assessment is not necessarily a test. A criterion-referenced test can be summative, but not all summative assessments are criterion-referenced tests. Authentic assessment is an example of formative assessment, yet formative assessment can be designed in different formats. Additionally, definitions are open to perspective and interpretation by researchers and educators alike. These examples illustrate the case in point: Defining the key subtleties between the different ways we assess student learning will help us to use each to their maximum effectiveness.

We understand there is an enormous amount of jargon regarding testing, but it is imperative to understand the purpose of each type of assessment. There is a time and place for all forms of assessment whether it is formative or summative but how do we as professionals determine that purpose? Most of us would agree that true *assessment* is the *complete array* of activities we perform with students. It is what we use on a daily basis to get a clear picture of what each student knows and is able to do as opposed to a test that is only one type of assessment. We need to differentiate between an assessment and a test and determine when it is appropriate to use each tool. How do we use continuous assessment throughout the year to inform our instruction?

In today's schools you will most likely hear discussions of teachers using both formative and summative assessments to track student progress. In the book *Classroom Assessment for Student Learning: Doing it Right—Using it Well* (Stiggins, Arter, Chappuis, & Chappuis, 2004) summative assessment is best described as the assessment *of* learning. This type of assessment usually occurs "after learning is supposed to have occurred to determine if it did" (Stiggins et al., p. 31). In contrast, formative assessment is referred to as the assessment *for* learning. Unlike summative assessment, formative assessment "happens while learning is still underway; that we conduct throughout teaching and learning to diagnose student needs, plan our next steps for instruction, provides students with feedback that they can use to improve the quality of their work" (Stiggins et al., p. 31). Yet, although educators may be saying the words we want to hear and abiding by the same definitions, upon closer introspect, we realize that there is still not a universal understanding of what formative assessment looks like in the classroom. Most formative assessment is still coming in test format, and in many cases what educators believe is a formative assessment is really summative.

Additionally, when we give a formative "test" as an assessment, it is only one piece of the assessment puzzle. One isolated task is not nearly enough information to give us a complete picture of what students know and are able to do. Wiggins and McTighe describe assessment as "the umbrella term for the deliberate use of many methods of gathering evidence of meeting desired results" (p. 6). Because many of the different types of tests and assessments overlap in their descriptions, we define the word *assessment* to be the full range of procedures used to gain information about student learning.

Hence it is vital that we explore a variety of ways that students can demonstrate their understanding of a skill or concept using various types of assessment. The key idea is that we are constantly assessing what we are teaching. When we continue teaching without stopping to assess along the way, we lose multiple opportunities to reteach, differentiate, clarify, or provide interventions. Lastly, once we have assessed students either formally, or informally, we need to know what to do with the data we collect. If students aren't learning, we need to address any difficulty as soon as possible, and do something different than we did the first time.

What we do different is the catch. Consider doing the following activity with your fellow team members or with your entire staff. This activity will help teachers narrow their focus and streamline the use of assessment in their classrooms. It will help to reduce the layers of "testing" that have overwhelmed teachers for years. By examining pitfalls of assessment and implications for instruction, teachers will become skilled at setting achievable goals, planning, pacing, and providing appropriate intervention as opposed to remediation.

Reduce the Layers of Assessment

Step 1: Write Down Tests

Acknowledging that most of the assessment that currently occurs in classrooms is given in the form of a test, the first step in reducing the layers of assessment is to identify all of these different tests given to students throughout the year. This process can be completed by an individual teacher, but is much more powerful when done as a grade-level or content-area team. When brainstorming this list, be sure to include all of the state-level tests, district-level tests, and classroom-level tests. Think about not only the common assessments across your team, but also the quizzes and individual "checks" that each teacher gives to the students in each classroom. When we start to look at the overwhelming number of tests that are given each year, it is easy to see why educators think that they don't have enough time to teach.

After writing down all of the tests you can think of that you give to students each year, you should end up with a chart that looks something like Figure 1.2 (page 6).

Figure 1.2. Chart of Tests

State Standards Tests Math	Math Text Chapter 10	Math District Assessment T2	Reading Text Theme 5	Writing Prompt Genre #3	Social Studies Midterm
State Standards Tests ELA	Math Text Chapter 11	Math District Assessment T3	Reading Text Theme 6	Writing Prompt Benchmark T1	Social Studies Final
Math Text Chapter 1	Math Text Chapter 12	English Learner State Test	Reading Text Theme 7	Writing Prompt Benchmark T2	Science Text Chapter 1
Math Text Chapter 2	Math Text Chapter 13	Reading Fluency Baseline	Reading Text Theme 8	Writing Prompt Benchmark T3	Science Text Chapter 2
Math Text Chapter 3	Math Text Chapter 14	Reading Fluency T1	Reading Text Theme 9	Social Studies Chapter 1	Science Text Chapter 3
Math Text Chapter 4	Math Text Chapter 15	Reading Fluency T2	Reading Text Theme 10	Social Studies Chapter 2	Science Text Chapter 4
Math Text Chapter 5	Math Text Unit 1	Reading Fluency T3	Summative Reading T1	Social Studies Chapter 3	Science Text Chapter 5
Math Text Chapter 6	Math Text Unit 2	Reading Text Theme 1	Summative Reading T2	Social Studies Chapter 4	Science Text Chapter 6
Math Text Chapter 7	Math Text Unit 3	Reading Text Theme 2	Summative Reading T3	Social Studies Chapter 5	Science Text Chapter 7
Math Text Chapter 8	Math Text Unit 4	Reading Text Theme 3	Writing Prompt Genre #1	Social Studies Chapter 6	Science Text Midterm
Math Text Chapter 9	Math District Assessment T1	Reading Text Theme 4	Writing Prompt Genre #2	Social Studies Chapter 7	Science Text Final

Step 2: Highlight Nonnegotiables

Knowing that we don't have complete control over the type or number of tests that we give students, the next step in this process is to begin sorting through the lists and determine which of the regularly given tests are nonnegotiable. For example, we know that all public schools are subject to the *No Child Left Behind* federal requirements for assuring that all children are meeting achievement standards. The *No Child Left Behind Act of 2001* requires annual testing for each state. States have flexibility in testing practice of whether to create criterion- or norm-referenced exams. In addition, there is variance between states as to which tests are given which years to select grade levels. Yet despite the varying testing requirements across the nation, each state requires that standardized tests be given to all students at a designated time in the year as part of this regulation.

Likewise, district tests are often designed as ways to track progress by trimester. Perhaps your district has also set common assessments at time intervals that everyone must give to their students such as a trimester math assessment or an end of term final. These tests, either centrally created or curriculum embedded, are used to provide benchmark data to districts. These tests, like the state tests, are usually nonnegotiable for teachers and students alike. These are the tests that absolutely need to be given, and they need to be set aside as we finish this layer of reduction.

Typically, the nonnegotiable tests are the summative tests. These are the tests that help to measure program effectiveness. They answer questions such as: How effective is the curriculum that is being used in the classroom? How effective is any given department or grade level? Summative tests are typically given at the end of a chapter or unit of instruction and help to define which students made it or didn't. These are the "dipstick" measures of how the students in a particular classroom did on a specific unit of study. These tools become an assessment "of" learning.

More often than not summative test results are recorded and we move on. This is not to imply however that summative tests have no place in our education system, they absolutely do. They help to provide equity in program delivery to all students. This type of assessment can be used to provide a starting point for collaboration between and among educators, and ensure that grade levels and departments are addressing the standards that are necessary for success for all students.

In contrast, formative assessments in the classroom tend to measure more of the individual student's knowledge. They are the benchmark assessments that occur during instruction. Formative assessments are the things that are being done on a daily basis to get an understanding of whether or not students are learning the skills that are being taught. Formative assessments provide the real time, immediate feedback that is so critical to the success of all learners. We now have a tool that is used as an assessment "for" learning. When used correctly, formative assessments are given in small steps along the way as pieces of a larger assessment process in which the sum of the information is used to guide our instruction.

Having highlighted the nonnegotiables, your chart should now look something like Figure 1.3 (page 9).

Figure 1.3. Nonnegotiable Tests

State Standards Tests Math	Math Text Chapter 10	**Math District Assessment T2**	Reading Text Theme 5	**Writing Prompt Genre #3**	Social Studies Midterm
State Standards Tests ELA	Math Text Chapter 11	**Math District Assessment T3**	Reading Text Theme 6	Writing Prompt Benchmark T1	Social Studies Final
Math Text Chapter 1	Math Text Chapter 12	**English Learner State Test**	Reading Text Theme 7	Writing Prompt Benchmark T2	Science Text Chapter 1
Math Text Chapter 2	Math Text Chapter 13	Reading Fluency Baseline	Reading Text Theme 8	Writing Prompt Benchmark T3	Science Text Chapter 2
Math Text Chapter 3	Math Text Chapter 14	Reading Fluency T1	Reading Text Theme 9	Social Studies Chapter 1	Science Text Chapter 3
Math Text Chapter 4	Math Text Chapter 15	Reading Fluency T2	Reading Text Theme 10	Social Studies Chapter 2	Science Text Chapter 4
Math Text Chapter 5	Math Text Unit 1	Reading Fluency T3	**Summative Reading T1**	Social Studies Chapter 3	Science Text Chapter 5
Math Text Chapter 6	Math Text Unit 2	Reading Text Theme 1	**Summative Reading T2**	Social Studies Chapter 4	Science Text Chapter 6
Math Text Chapter 7	Math Text Unit 3	Reading Text Theme 2	**Summative Reading T3**	Social Studies Chapter 5	Science Text Chapter 7
Math Text Chapter 8	Math Text Unit 4	Reading Text Theme 3	**Writing Prompt Genre #1**	Social Studies Chapter 6	Science Text Midterm
Math Text Chapter 9	**Math District Assessment T1**	Reading Text Theme 4	**Writing Prompt Genre #2**	Social Studies Chapter 7	Science Text Final

Step 3: Toss Out Additional Summative Tests

You now have two sets of assessments to look at, those that are mandated and those that you have some control over. If we look only at the nonnegotiables, they alone are not overwhelming. In fact, if these are the only mandates, then technically we are only required to test a few times a year. That begs the question: Why does it seem like we are always testing our students? If we answer this question honestly, we see the rationale for this step in our reduction process.

You are ready to look at the tests that are optional and sort this group one more time. This time divide the remaining tests into summative versus formative assessments. When deciding which group to put them in, remember to refer to the working definitions of each term.

You will undoubtedly observe that there are already many nonnegotiable tests identified, and the majority of these tests are most likely in a summative format. Thus, you probably have enough tests built into your program that will give you the tracking information you need throughout the year. So, once you have identified the remaining summative tests (i.e., those that are not mandatory), we recommend that you toss most of them out of your repertoire. Keep only those summative tests that give you information about your program or students that is not provided by the nonnegotiable summative tests.

By reducing the amount of summative tests that we give students, we can focus our efforts more on formative data. Unlike summative assessments that provide the snapshots of learning at one moment in time, formative assessments help to form the big picture of student learning so that by the time you get to the end of a unit of study you have a clear understanding of all the components involved in that particular students overall ability. Formative assessment helps with evidence-based instructional decision making. It helps to provide the information a teacher needs to make any changes to instruction on a daily basis (Popham, 2008).

After tossing out the additional nonessential summative tests, you should begin to see a reduction in the amount of tests you give to students similar to the chart in Figure 1.4 (page 11).

Figure 1.4. After Tossing Out Additional Summative Tests

State Standards Tests Math	Math Text Chapter 10	**Math District Assessment T2**		**Writing Prompt Genre #3**	
State Standards Tests ELA	Math Text Chapter 11	**Math District Assessment T3**		Writing Prompt Benchmark T1	
Math Text Chapter 1	Math Text Chapter 12	**English Learner State Test**		Writing Prompt Benchmark T2	Science Text Chapter 1
Math Text Chapter 2	Math Text Chapter 13	Reading Fluency Baseline		Writing Prompt Benchmark T3	Science Text Chapter 2
Math Text Chapter 3	Math Text Chapter 14	Reading Fluency T1		Social Studies Chapter 1	Science Text Chapter 3
Math Text Chapter 4	Math Text Chapter 15	Reading Fluency T2		Social Studies Chapter 2	Science Text Chapter 4
Math Text Chapter 5		Reading Fluency T3	**Summative Reading T1**	Social Studies Chapter 3	Science Text Chapter 5
Math Text Chapter 6			**Summative Reading T2**	Social Studies Chapter 4	Science Text Chapter 6
Math Text Chapter 7			**Summative Reading T3**	Social Studies Chapter 5	Science Text Chapter 7
Math Text Chapter 8			**Writing Prompt Genre #1**	Social Studies Chapter 6	
Math Text Chapter 9	**Math District Assessment T1**		**Writing Prompt Genre #2**	Social Studies Chapter 7	

Step 4: Reduce Formative "Tests"

Historically, textbooks are organized by chapters, units, and themes of sorts. At the end of each, there is a test for teachers to give to "assess" how well the students understood the content. This system, as well intended as it is, does not accommodate for the refinement of instruction and the mastery of student learning. Often the "tests" are lengthy to administer and take the teacher a considerable amount of time to grade and record. By the time the students are given feedback on the test, rigorous pacing guides force the teacher to "move on" to the next unit of study.

Even in best-case scenarios where a teacher takes students through an error analysis of a test, and cyclical review is built into the curriculum, more time is spent covering the material than allowing students multiple opportunities to learn and truly understand the content. As a result, these formative tests act more as summative tests and become nothing more than a percentage in the grade book to be averaged up at report card time. So why do teachers feel obligated to give every chapter test? Could a student do a project on the Byzantine Empire in social studies as opposed to spending an entire class period taking the chapter embedded test? Could a teacher teach multiplication facts through ten without giving a test after each fact taught? Would it be possible to show understanding of chemical reactions in science through a lab practical as opposed to a test? If you answered *yes* to any of the above questions, then you are beginning to see the point.

Take some time to look at your chapter tests to see where alternatives could be implemented or where concepts can be combined. Then toss out the extra formative tests that only add to the overwhelming and unnecessary testing of your students. Your chart should now look like Figure 1.5 (page 13).

Figure 1.5. After Tossing Out Additional Formative Tests

State Standards Tests Math		Math District Assessment T2		Writing Prompt Genre #3	
State Standards Tests ELA		Math District Assessment T3			
	Math Text Chapter 12	English Learner State Test			
		Reading Fluency Baseline			
Math Text Chapter 3		Reading Fluency T1			Science Text Chapter 3
	Math Text Chapter 15	Reading Fluency T2			
		Reading Fluency T3	Summative Reading T1	Social Studies Chapter 3	
Math Text Chapter 6			Summative Reading T2		Science Text Chapter 6
			Summative Reading T3		
			Writing Prompt Genre #1	Social Studies Chapter 6	
Math Text Chapter 9	Math District Assessment T1		Writing Prompt Genre #2		

Step 5: Replace Reduced Formative "Tests" With Other Types of Assessment

You are now left with a list of formative assessments some of which are in the form of "tests" and others that may be activity or observation based. Although we are trying to reduce the layers of assessment, it is important to acknowledge that we are not advocating elimination of assessment. Instead, we support replacing "tests" with other ways of gathering the same assessment data. In upcoming chapters, you will learn how tools such as verification logs, rubrics, and goal-tracking sheets can provide teachers with useful information of student learning without ever administering a test. Once you are familiar with each tool, you will want to decide where you will use tools like these to gather the same information that you once attempted to get through endless testing measures. Your final chart will then look much like Figure 1.6 (page 15).

Summary

Although we must acknowledge that all types of assessments have their appropriate time and place in education, we can't lose focus of the reason why we assess student learning. We must remember that "quality classroom assessment produces accurate information that is used effectively to maximize student learning" (Stiggins et al., 2004, p. 26). Stiggins, Arter, Chappuis, and Chappuis are telling us that the importance of assessment is to inform our instruction on a day-to-day basis so as to maximize student learning, which leads us back to the purpose of this book: effective use of formative assessment.

If we return to the question posed at the beginning of this chapter and concentrate on the real reason for assessing students, we will be able to refocus our approach to the whole assessment process. True formative assessment that occurs on a daily basis, minute by minute in the classroom, provides us, in our role as educators, with a constant compass for student learning. We are able to remap our instructional direction so as to reach the target in the most efficient way. Assessment does not need to be in the form of a test, but should revolve around the data of daily practice and the insight that our professional experiences allow us to gain.

Figure 1.6. The Final Chart

State Standards Tests Math		**Math District Assessment T2**		**Writing Prompt Genre #3**	
State Standards Tests ELA		**Math District Assessment T3**			
	Math Text Chapter 12	**English Learner State Test**	Evidence Collections		
Verification Logs		Reading Fluency Baseline		Rubrics	
Math Text Chapter 3		Reading Fluency T1			Science Text Chapter 3
	Math Text Chapter 15	Reading Fluency T2			
		Reading Fluency T3	**Summative Reading T1**	Social Studies Chapter 3	
Math Text Chapter 6		Repeated Reading Charts	**Summative Reading T2**		Science Text Chapter 6
	Goal-Tracking Sheets		**Summative Reading T3**	Group Projects	
			Writing Prompt Genre #1	Social Studies Chapter 6	Lab Practicals
Math Text Chapter 9	**Math District Assessment T1**		**Writing Prompt Genre #2**		

2

Applying Data—
What's Stopping Us?

Never has there been a better educational acronym than DuFour's *DRIP*—Data Rich, Information Poor (2005). What more appropriate way to describe the abundance of statistical data available to educators bogging us down from getting to the nitty-gritty of student achievement? After all, there is hardly an educator out there who would argue that he or she does not have access to enough data. Instead, the educator would most likely attest that he or she is drowning in it. With so much being thrown at us, it is easy to understand why many can't find a starting point. We know we need to do something, but we are frozen in regards to what action to take.

Which, of course, begs the questions: Is it possible that the "knowing versus doing" gap that we often attribute to students is really our own gap? If so, how do we attempt to close it? We must first invest in developing our leadership and capacity. The mere fact that you are reading this book is testament to your leadership, and what you will learn as a result will be the capacity to teach others. We must bring others along through effective collaboration as we continue to hone our own skills as well as the skills of our teams and staffs. We need to figure out what to do with the data we have and then use it to improve instruction and learning.

We've all heard the popular colloquialism of "using data to drive our instruction." But what does that really mean? If data is shared, and used correctly, it can help teachers change their pedagogy and improve their craft. Effective use of data will help us to both inform our instruction and to differentiate that instruction to meet the needs of all of our students. We will be better equipped to know when to move on in our instructional plan or to slow down to ensure that all students are mastering the particular standard being addressed. As we engage in a system of inquiry around this data with our colleagues and students, thoughtful analysis and reflection of effective data use will help us to know what to drop from our plates or identify what to emphasize in our instruction.

We've found ways to collect data and print out beautiful bar graphs that demonstrate that students are "low in vocabulary." On the surface, this sounds great, but how does what we say translate into the classroom? Many successful teachers innately operate in a system of constant refinement of instruction until their students can produce a desired level of success. Yet articulating the steps to this success continues to remain a mystery to the masses. We have lost sight of the basic elements of good teaching and instructional refinement.

So let's go back and outline those basic elements by starting with the definitions and purpose for each type of data that we collect. When we look at state and district data, we have data that, when analyzed, provides us with summative trends to guide formative decisions. Because we are looking for trends at this level, combined with the fact that this data will not stay current long enough to influence ongoing decisions, belaboring this type of data will not lead to the kind of action directly correlated to student achievement. This data should be used to set long-term goals and then put aside and reviewed at future benchmark checkpoints.

Likewise, school level data, although important, is too far removed for day-to-day decision making. This type of data analysis leads to using summative data to identify focus areas. We use our schoolwide data and compare it to our state and district trends to map out what we need to teach. These focus areas become our measures of student achievement and provide us a checklist of what we need to teach and reteach until all students can demonstrate mastery.

How we monitor that brings us closer to a type of data that we should keep at hand, which is grade-level data. Analysis of grade-level data helps us use summative and formative data to align and refine teaching practices. This is extremely important when we look at things such as pacing and planning and in depth or cursory levels of instruction, as well as goal setting, discreet skill building, and extensions of learning.

But what truly has the greatest impact, and the data where the most action occurs, is at the classroom level. Classroom data analysis leads to action! The majority of this data should be formative so that it can be used to teach, assess, and refine the abilities of students.

Finding examples of effective data use can be like finding a needle in a haystack. It is imperative to remember that to be at the highest level of effectiveness, data must be complete and timely. We must also remember that we have several different types of data to use when making decisions about our teaching. Obviously the data that is directly related to student learning is going to have the greatest influence.

If we look at the system top down from the state and district, school to team to classroom levels, we find we are doing many wonderful things with data. However, with this approach we often run out of steam before we get to the level that creates the biggest impact. To simplify the process, perhaps we need to reexamine our approach, begin with a smaller data set, and work backwards. Once we master what that means for our own group at the classroom level, we will be able to create consistency among our teams, and finally move together as a uniform school group toward a common goal.

Consider the most common method for analyzing data seen in schools today. Administrators attend summer workshops at the district level to receive and analyze state testing data for their school. They spend hours organizing the information into comprehensible charts to present to teachers on the first day back to school. Teachers then confront the fear of failure or the joy of success, depending on how their group did and how well the school did overall. As a staff, teachers and administrators draw conclusions and set overarching goals that everyone agrees to strive for over the next school year. Administrators then use those goals as a focus for classroom observations for the next ten months.

But for years great educational researchers, authors, and staff developers have been advocating for a more concentrated approach to making data more comprehensible. With the notion of professional learning communities, we are forced to continue our work beyond the first week back to school. Looking at bits and pieces of data in isolation leads to weakened instruction and ineffective intervention because of fragmented instruction. Therefore, the movement calls for regular meetings and focused articulation around goals and achievement.

In Nancy Love's book, *The Data Coach's Guide to Improving Learning for All Students* (2004), she asserts that, "Schools are gathering more and more data, but having data available does not mean that data are used to guide instructional improvement. Many schools lack the process to connect the data that they have with the results they must produce" (p. 16). If data is to be truly useful, then teachers must be able to determine what data to look at. Teachers need to be given the tools and strategies to be able to formulate questions to guide their own reflection around the data. And administrators must build time in to the schedule for authentic collaboration among and between teachers and grade levels.

Larry Ainsworth (2003) teaches us the importance of "unwrapping the standards" to clearly define what exactly it is we want students to learn. Richard DuFour (2005) outlines for us a process of setting SMART goals that are measurable and achievable. Rick Stiggins (2004) helps us to evaluate the effectiveness of our common formative assessments and illustrates how we can create our own. Mike Schmoker (1999) shows us how to articulate our process through the simple steps of a structured team meeting. And Doug Reeves (2008) and Robert Marzano (2006) challenge us to reexamine our grading and reporting policies to reflect the true abilities of students. With so many great minds at work, and processes so clearly outlined, why do we continue to see a hodgepodge of hit-or-miss approaches still at work?

The solution may be easier than we think. Being an educator in this time of high-stakes accountability is exhausting. Ask any teacher if he believes he has enough time to teach the required content to the level that all students succeed, and you will most likely be answered with a hearty chuckle. Compound that lack of time with inflexible adherence to rigorous pacing guides; a demand to thoroughly understand adopted core curriculum; daily, weekly, monthly, and yearly planning; seemingly endless grading of assignments; state and district testing mandates; recording grades and reporting to parents; adjunct duties; and obligatory staff meetings (just to name a few of the things that demand our time) and it is no wonder that teachers do not have time for the most difficult, albeit the most essential, work.

Consider Bob, for example. Bob has been teaching fifth grade for the past seventeen years. He has experienced pendulum shifts from whole language, to direct explicit instruction, and everything in between. Today's high-stakes accountability is certainly not "how it used to be" for Bob. His school is considered underperforming and Bob's state test scores are the lowest of his team for the fourth year in a row.

In September, Bob returns from summer vacation and attends the beginning-of-the-year staff meeting. He listens as his principal presents last spring's state testing data broken down by school, grade level, subject, and strand. Teams brainstorm together to identify strengths and weaknesses to share out to the faculty. Bob learns that in English language arts, the school needs to focus on comprehension, his team on vocabulary, and he as a teacher on writing applications. Bob then receives his class list and learns that last year's fourth graders were lowest in writing applications. A similar process occurs for math.

Bob arrives at school on time and is assigned morning duty every other week. He spends his time after school grading papers and planning lessons for six different content areas for the next day. He is a member of the teacher's union and is assigned to the character education committee as his adjunct duty. He is willing to put in time beyond his contract hours, but Bob also coaches his daughter's softball team and is actively involved in his church.

Fortunately, Bob teaches at a school with weekly, modified days built into the schedule for collaboration. Throughout the year, Bob attends monthly staff meetings in which the principal brings current benchmark data to analyze and compare to the school's reading comprehension goal. At their biweekly staff meetings, Bob's team focuses on improving academic vocabulary instruction and sharing work samples, successes, and struggles. At the last collaboration meeting of the month, Bob attends professional development with a focus determined by the principal.

Unfortunately, Bob doesn't have much time leftover to focus on his own areas of need. Feeling the pressure of being the lowest-achieving teacher, Bob tries to figure out what to do. He isn't sure whether he should focus on writing strategies, his weakest area, or writing applications, the weakest area of his current students (or so he assumes). In addition, he doesn't know what he needs to do to make the necessary changes and doesn't have either the time or the opportunity to receive the training he needs. And that is just for language arts. What is Bob to do?

Of course, setting a common course and ensuring articulation along the way are certainly critical components to staying on track and moving in the right direction. We are not suggesting letting these important practices fall by the wayside. Instead, we advocate for shifting our priorities to allot more time for teachers to understand data at the most basic level. To use classroom data to answer simple questions such as, "Are students learning?" and "How do I know?"

Schools moving in this direction would foster articulation to help teachers to clearly identify students meeting expectations and those needing extra support. In addition, teachers would have the time to identify the causes of such struggles and devise plans that would address solutions. This system would cease to make time the constant and learning subjective to the timeline. Instead, time would become the variable, and students would be given multiple opportunities to demonstrate learning in a multitude of ways. Data would come in various forms not just fancy printouts from summative tests. Tests, rubrics, goal-tracking sheets, evidence collections, and student verification logs would provide us with just some of the data needed to support decisions leading to improved instruction. As a result, true differentiation would occur and all students would experience success.

Summary

Being able to effectively organize and track data is not only helpful to teachers for the refinement of instruction, but also in reporting feedback to students and parents. It is important that schools discuss and define the purpose for collecting and reporting data to ensure consistency from teacher to teacher. To avoid misinterpretation, schools should explicitly define the purpose for each reporting tool used (Guskey & Bailey, 2001, p. 56).

Because teachers often use a body of evidence for reporting progress, the key to effective data analysis is to provide educators with a simple approach. The more we learn about best practices, the more complex the process becomes. Teachers and administrators overwhelmed by this complexity can become paralyzed and do less despite knowing more. Helping to define the "what," "why," and "when" of data analysis allows for a systematic approach. Figure 2.1 breaks the process down into uncomplicated terms.

Figure 2.1. A Systematic Approach

Type of Data	Purpose	Frequency Monitoring
State and District	◆ Summative trends to guide formative decisions	Once a year Trimester benchmarks
Schoolwide	◆ Set vision ◆ Decide on instructional focus ◆ Implications for professional development	Several times a year
Grade Level	◆ PLC work ◆ Bridge between school and classroom goals	Several times a trimester
Classroom	◆ Check for student learning ◆ Provide individual student support ◆ Refinement of instruction	Daily, weekly, ongoing

"Analyzing data enables teachers to understand student learning needs more clearly and therefore be able to address those needs through classroom instruction. When teachers know how to determine the gaps in student learning, they use laser-like focus in teaching to address those gaps so students progress toward rigorous, content-specific standards" (Hirsh & Killion, 2007, p. 67).

3

Streamlining the Assessment Process— Identifying Learning Objectives

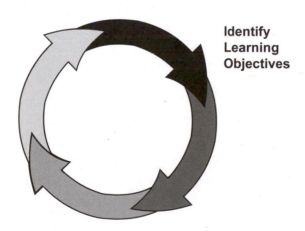

Identify Learning Objectives

When we identify our learning objective, we first ask ourselves the question, "What should students know and be able to do?" We can do that by identifying key standards or key learning goals. You might even hear this referred to as benchmark goals that are itemized as report card descriptors. Whatever the terminology, we must decide what the ultimate goal for student learning is and, when we are done teaching, what evidence will we have that will demonstrate that students have learned the intended objective.

Of course, good instruction is also a key factor in quality output. The what, how, and why we teach is extremely important. However, our best teaching is merely the blueprint and tools needed to achieve a product. Think of baking a cake. To bake a delicious cake, quality ingredients are imperative. It is also essential that we carefully follow the recipe and be skilled at measuring and modifying when needed. Lastly, we must use appropriate materials and stick to specific time frames. Yet, when your guests arrive, they will not consider any of the above. The only thing your guests will consider is the final product: *How does the cake taste?* Thus, preparation and procedures affect an outcome, but the outcome is really the bottom line.

In his book, *Transformative Assessment* (2008), James Popham defines instruction as "the set of teacher-determined activities carried out in an effort to get students to accomplish a curricular outcome." (p. 50). He goes on to explain that instruction, however motivating or carefully planned, is only the means to helping students achieve that outcome and not a form of assessment. Therefore, when we refer to the assessment piece in this chapter, we are speaking only of the student output. In addition, formative assessment allows teachers to know when adjustments must be made to their instruction.

When designing activities and assignments for our students, we must keep the focus on identifying what the students know and are able to do. Then, we must constantly look at the purpose behind the activity we are asking students to complete. Coupled together, we will begin to find ways to gain learning information about students without putting another test in front of them. This is just one way teachers can reduce the layers of formative assessment in the classroom.

Looking through this lens of assessment, we can help reduce the layers and free up time in our classroom by using many of our classroom assignments as a way of assessing student learning. Thus, if we look at our learning objectives before students are engaged in academic work, the student output should demonstrate the learned objective. At the most basic level, looking at student work samples is a great way to illustrate this point. When reviewing the following examples, are the learning goals evident in the end products? Do they tell us what students know and are able to do? Do they indicate what the learning objective was? And based on that information, should we keep these assignments, modify them to better match our learning goals, or toss them out of the rotation completely?

Figure 3.1. Kindergarten Writing Assignment

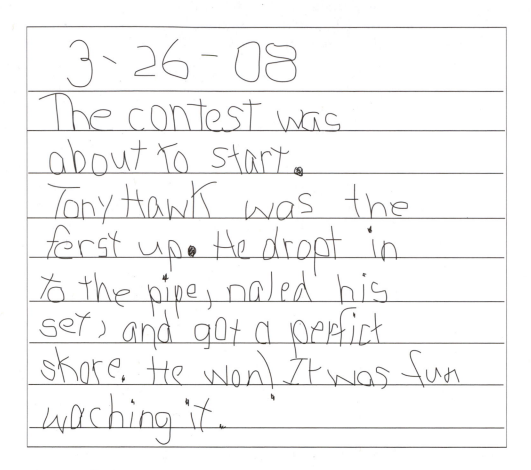

Keep, Modify, or Toss?

From looking at the work sample in Figure 3.1, one can see that the student can write a simple paragraph with a topic sentence, supporting sentences, and a conclusion. Depending on the grade level, we can determine if this is sufficient to meet the expectation benchmark, or if the child needs further instruction. Knowing that this child is a kindergartner, and using the benchmark that students will write three patterned sentences to a given topic, we can see that the student has clearly surpassed the assignment goal. We can also identify exactly what the child knows and what the next step in instruction might be. Having this assignment as an assessment, the teacher can now extend the student's learning beyond grade-level standards by focusing on standard spelling, higher-level vocabulary, and compound sentence building. Therefore, we would recommend keeping this assignment as a way of assessing student learning.

Now consider the next example, and again ask yourself if the learning goal is evident in the end product. Do we have evidence that the student has learned that goal?

Figure 3.2. Sixth Grade Social Studies Assignment

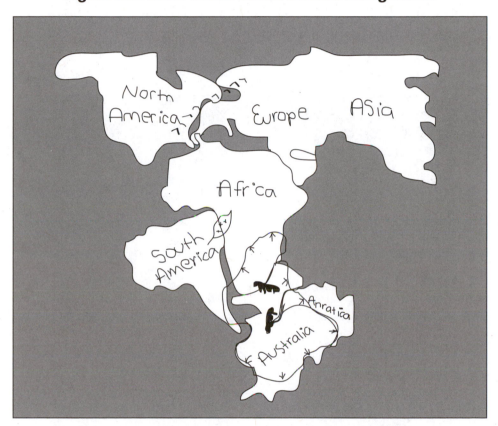

At first glance, it is difficult to determine the exact objective of this assignment. Is it to identify and layout the seven continents? Would you keep, modify, or toss it? Would knowing that this was the output of a sixth grade class change your perspective? Seeing the connecting mountain ranges might give us yet another clue that this assignment had something to do with the ancient Greek supercontinent of Pangaea. So what exactly was the objective and how do we know if this child is successful?

In this sample, we might recommend keeping the assignment, but modifying it so it more clearly indicates the desired learning. For example, just adding a title, labels, and a key to the map would more clearly illustrate what the student had learned from this lesson. Is this assignment merely to demonstrate what Pangaea might have looked like? Or might the teacher want to elicit a deeper understanding where the student outlines how Pangaea was formed citing fossil evidence that proves Pangaea may have actually existed? Perhaps students should be required to explain hypotheses such as the Continental Drift Theory that caused the break up of the continent? In the latter case, is this assignment rigorous enough to demonstrate the level of understanding required of an assessment? If not, could it be modified to serve these purposes?

Finally, consider the example shown in Figure 3.3.

Figure 3.3. Third Grade Noodle Man Assignment

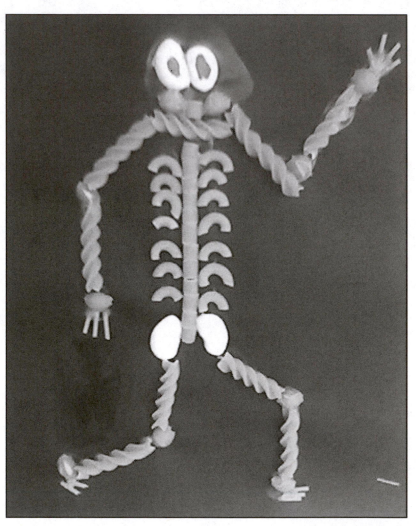

We fondly refer to this assignment as *noodle man*. Noodle man is adorable and no doubt was fun to make, but in the end does he demonstrate student learning? Is this a lesson of the human skeletal system? There are 12 pairs of ribs in the human body for a total of 24, yet noodle man only has 14. The human vertebral column consists of 33 vertebrae; noodle man only has 12 vertebrae. What might noodle man look like if all his ribs and vertebrae were represented? Would it represent a clear proportional picture of the human skeletal system, or a distorted image based on the size of the noodles being used?

Perhaps this student is demonstrating a lack of understanding on this assignment, but we cannot be sure without knowing the intent of the assignment. Having seen a class output of noodle man proudly displayed at Halloween time, it would be safe to assume that noodle man was nothing more than a fun holiday activity. Knowing that, it raises an important question for educators: *When instructional time is at a premium, can we dedicate an hour of our time with only noodle man to show for our efforts?*

At times this is a difficult fact for teachers to face. But, in the interest of simplifying the overwhelming state of education, sometimes we just need to toss out the bear unit. This is not to say that we cannot have fun at school. For example, we could use noodles in our third grade classroom to introduce proper use of commas and quotation marks. Or, we could create skeletons for Halloween, but insist that they be anatomically correct. We would recommend having grade-level conversations to determine fun assignments that would align with benchmark goals. This would be a wise investment of time so that the temptation was not there to provide variety by throwing in time-wasting activities.

To ensure quality lessons and activities, teachers could mold their practice using the structure outlined in Jay McTighe and Grant Wiggins *Understanding By Design* (1998) model. In their "Backwards Design" illustration, McTighe and Wiggins delineate three stages to curriculum planning:

Stage #1: Identify desired results

Stage #2: Determine acceptable evidence

Stage #3: Plan learning experiences and instruction

"The backward design orientation suggests that we think about our design in terms of collected evidence needed to document and validate that the desired results have been achieved" (p. 12).

If learning objectives are identified before students are engaged in academic work, then student output should demonstrate learned objectives. Thus another good investment of time would be to recreate a work collection analysis in a school wide staff meeting to be sure that the *Understanding By Design* process has occurred. Teachers can objectively look at student work samples to determine if the assignment indicates what a student knows and is able to do, and what is the desired learning objective of each assignment. Begin by using neutral samples (may be borrowed from another school) to ensure nonbiased discussion. Then, follow these simple steps:

1. Review the purpose of the activity to learn how to critically look at work we give students to evaluate its usefulness in assessing student learning.

2. Pose the following questions to the group. For each assignment, does the student output tell us what the student knows and is able to do? Does it indicate the learning objective? Should it be kept, modified, or tossed?

3. Pass out three different colored index cards to each participant to indicate *keep, modify,* and *toss.*

4. Using a document camera or computer slide show, display various samples of student work from multiple grade levels. Remind teachers to look at assignments through the lens of assessment.

5. As each assignment is displayed, have teachers vote on the value of assignments based on grade-level benchmarks by raising one of the three cards in their hands. When teachers raise their colored cards, scan to see if they are in agreement. If not, poll the group to determine the reasoning behind the difference of opinion.

6. Keep working until the staff begins to reach consensus the majority of the time.

7. Revisit the process throughout the year by infusing anonymous work samples from your own site or work in grade-level teams where each teacher brings two or three work samples to be analyzed by the group.

By engaging in this continuous analysis and discussion, teachers will begin to prioritize the work they give to students. In addition, they will find that they have more time for reteaching and differentiating instruction because they are not bogging down in senseless activities or unnecessary tests. Likewise, they will find that they are creating ways to channel fun activities while making them purposeful at the same time.

We believe teachers should always identify the learning objective for students especially as the students get older. This does not mean that we ignore the essential standards that we have previously identified but we use those standards to guide our students toward their own learning goals. We facilitate a clear understanding of the objectives by putting them in student friendly language. When students are taught how to use self-generated rubrics they can begin to self assess their own progress toward attaining those goals. Using SMART goals is another way to involve students in monitoring their own progress. This process helps to identify specific learning targets for each individual student. SMART goals are designed to be specific, measurable, attainable, results oriented, and time bound. Teachers can begin the practice of using SMART goals with their students by writing the goals themselves. As the students become more familiar and comfortable with their own learning, they can write their own goals. The ultimate outcome is that we put students in charge of their learning by guiding and directing them down an appropriate path based on accurate and timely assessment data. This path is different for each student and is carefully planned to be the most efficient route to the final destination of achievement and success. If we get into the habit of identifying the objectives for ourselves as educators we will have a clear picture of where we're going. We will have a well-defined map of our year, and a process to collect plenty of evidence that demonstrates what our students know and are able to do. We can then report that evidence to the parents and our colleagues, in addition to having a real tool to inform our instruction along the way. We can still have fun with some of our favorite activities but they are no longer just activities, they become a purposeful assignment giving us assessment information about student learning.

Summary

A current reality in some districts is that all assessments must be aligned in format to the standardized tests. However, it doesn't mean that you need to give students a test every time you want to assess their learning. By having clearly defined objectives in every lesson, you can present the class or homework assignment and achieve multiple outcomes simultaneously. You have taught the lesson, provided time for independent practice, and are able to align the content through daily practice. You are now assessing as you go so that when the students turn in their work, you have immediate feedback as to whether or not they understood the concept being taught. If they have mastered it, fantastic—move on to the next lesson. If not, you are able to adjust your teaching so as to provide multiple opportunities for success all without having to give students a formal test to measure their learning. Real-time feedback makes the largest impact on student learning.

Have you ever heard a student ask the question, "When am I ever going to need this information?" or make the statement that "This is a waste of my time." How many times have we asked ourselves, "How am I going to find time to do one more thing?" By assigning purposeful activities that allow students to demonstrate their knowledge and also give the teacher a direction for refining and adjusting instruction, the aforementioned questions no longer pose such a dilemma. Through careful and thoughtful collaboration, teachers across the grade level will be able to reach consensus as to what the critical skills are in each content area for each part of the school year. Likewise, students will have a clearer understanding of the purpose for their efforts. If we expect students to "buy-in" to and become actively engaged in their own learning, they deserve to know how the assignment, activity, or assessment is a critical part of their educational journey.

Benchmarks can be established that guide the curricular paths throughout the school year and into the next. No longer do we need to wait until the end of a grading period to determine which students have mastered the standards and then worry if some have not. With this approach, we are able to guide all students to higher levels of achievement.

4

Streamlining the Assessment Process—Collecting the Data

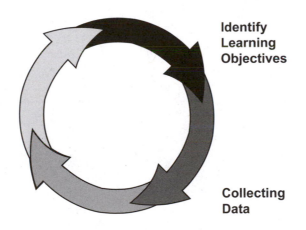

**Identify
Learning
Objectives**

**Collecting
Data**

This chapter takes our streamlining process one step further. Because we do not want to wait until the end of a chapter or a unit to give a test to see how students are doing, we must look at ways to collect data along the way. As we defined earlier, assessment does not refer to a single event in time. It is data collected over time that paints a picture of student progress and ultimately student success. This step of the process proposes ways in which to paint that picture using tools that are already somewhat familiar to us.

There is one important caveat. Although we may use familiar systems to collect data to systems you may have used in the past, these systems have been altered and refined to better serve formative assessment purposes. It is essential that educators do not overgeneralize these tools and slide into a pattern of using them the way they *used to*. One must approach these strategies with assessment in mind. They are to be used to collect evidence of student ability and performance. We are going to ask ourselves the question, "What evidence demonstrates what students know and are able to do?" And we are going to collect that information through a wide array of tools, including assignments, rubrics and scoring guides, goal-tracking sheets, verification logs, evidence collections, exit slips, and checklists.

These tools are just a few of the bountiful ways that teachers can collect data on student learning. We recommend using these ideas as a starter list to encourage moving away from traditional testing and collecting better evidence to better inform instruction. As you become more skillful in assessing without testing, you will expand this list to include other ways of checking for understanding such as oral language, projects, questions, and writing (Fisher & Frey, 2007). In addition, you may add ideas for gathering other types of formative data such as letter-card responses, key questioning during discussion, whiteboard responses, traffic signal technique, and item sampling (Popham, 2008, pp. 58–63). The ideas are infinite, it is the process that must be learned.

Rubrics

We've taken a detailed look at assignments and discussed how to more carefully plan lessons so that the output of each assignment can serve as a way of gathering data. Now, to demonstrate this process further, we explore yet another simple way to collect data: *rubrics*. Rubrics help us identify what kids know and are able to do because they act as a checklist. They help to determine the next steps for instruction by providing specific feedback toward goals. They also allow opportunity for student involvement so students can take that feedback, see where they need to focus, and set self-generated goals for themselves. Finally, rubrics outline quality criteria.

Figure 4.1 illustrates the general layout of a rubric.

Figure 4.1. General Layout of a Rubric

	Performance Level				
	Advanced 4	Proficient 3	Basic 2	Below 1	Score (1–4)
Target Objective #1	List of criteria that would demonstrate that the student went beyond the required objective.	List of criteria that would demonstrate that the student met the required objective.	List of criteria that would demonstrate that the student is moving toward the required objective.	List of criteria that would demonstrate that the student did not meet the required objective.	
Target Objective #2	Repeat list of criteria as outlined above.	Repeat...	Repeat...	Repeat...	
Target Objective #3	Repeat list of criteria as outlined above.	Repeat...	Repeat...	Repeat...	

Performance standards are listed across the top, and target objectives are listed down the side. It is helpful to limit each rubric to no more than three to four target objectives so as to keep assignments manageable. For each of the target objectives, criteria are listed indicating each specific level of accomplishment. All scores are added together for overall assessment results.

In most classrooms today, you are likely to find some evidence of rubric use. Typically, educators use rubrics to assess student writing, making the feedback more specific and less subjective. Still, rubrics could be used even more often—across all content areas. In fact, when rubrics are aligned with goals, students can help generate the criteria by which they will be required to demonstrate proficiency. These student-generated rubrics will clearly outline the objectives and tell students if they have achieved the goal. If so, they will have check marks for all criteria outlined in the "proficient" column of the rubric. When that is the case, students can look to the advanced column to see what they could work on to bring their work to a more advanced level. Conversely, if a student falls below the proficient column in any of the criteria, the student can decide where to focus his or her efforts so as to move toward a level of proficiency.

Teachers can also use rubrics to help guide students toward individual goals as well as determine next steps for instruction. Using a rubric, a teacher can specifically teach to the benchmark objectives and even provide samples of what expected output might look like. The example of Mrs. Johnson helps us better illustrate this point.

Mrs. Johnson sets the following learning objectives for her students:

Students will be able to—

♦ Locate information in reference texts.

♦ Understand information presented in reference texts.

♦ Apply various levels of questioning to demonstrate knowledge.

♦ Quote or paraphrase information sources, citing them appropriately.

♦ Write clear, coherent sentences and paragraphs that develop a central idea.

She assigns her fourth grade class a task to work in pairs and write an expository paragraph about a mammal. The students are to design a comprehension quiz to share with fellow classmates. The quiz must consist of at least five questions that encompass a range of questions from at least three various levels of Bloom's Taxonomy (Knowledge, Comprehension, Application, Analysis, Synthesis, and Evaluation). In addition, each set of partners must include an answer key with their quiz.

Mrs. Johnson then either teaches or reviews several lessons:

1. Since it is a third-grade standard in her school that third graders write a well-developed paragraph, Mrs. Johnson spends little time on the technical teaching of this aspect of the assignment with her current fourth graders. However, Mrs. Johnson thinks it would be wise to review the components of a good paragraph with her students to ensure that the final output contains all required elements.

2. Although her class has had some experience in applying research, Mrs. Johnson again models for her students how to gather and sort information that is relevant and irrelevant. She teaches them again how to paraphrase information into their own words. Lifting, quoting, and citing text are also a part of this lesson.

3. In addition, to be successful at the end of this lesson, students will need to be able to demonstrate that they understand the various levels of questioning and be able to apply it using Bloom's Taxonomy as a model. Because Mrs. Johnson has been focusing on Bloom's Taxonomy during her reading lessons, she only needs to remind her students of what questions might look like at each level. She asks her students to generate a list together to use as a guide during the assignment (Figure 4.2, page 40).

Figure 4.2. Question Examples from Bloom's Taxonomy

Knowledge	What is the mammal?	How would you describe this mammal?	What does this mammal do?
Comprehension	What evidence indicates that this mammal does...?	What was the cause of...?	Why does this mammal do...?
Application	How would this mammal act in a different environment?	In which sentence would this vocabulary term best fit?	If you were this mammal, what would you do?
Analysis	Which are the most important facts about this mammal?	What evidence indicates that this mammal...?	How would you compare this mammal with a...?
Synthesis	In what situation might this mammal need to...?	How would this mammal best be protected?	What would it be like to put a ... into this mammal's habitat?
Evaluation	Would you be happy being this type of mammal? Why?	What is the best thing about this mammal?	Is this mammal important? Justify your answer.

4. Finally, Mrs. Johnson provides her students with samples of different formats of questions that they could use in their quiz: multiple choice, fill in the blank, short answer, etc.

Together Mrs. Johnson and the class devise the rubric shown in Figure 4.3.

Figure 4.3. Rubric for Mammal Lesson

	Performance Level				Score (1–4)
	Advanced 4	**Proficient 3**	**Basic 2**	**Below 1**	
Composes Research-Based Paragraph About a Mammal	___ Students write multiple paragraphs ___ Paragraph includes more than three research-based detail sentences	___ Paragraph is complete with topic, details, & conclusion ___ Paragraph includes at least three research-based detail sentences ___ All research is paraphrased in students' own words	___ Paragraph is missing either the topic, details, or conclusion ___ Paragraph includes at least two research-based detail sentences ___ Some research is paraphrased in students' own words	___ Paragraph is missing majority of topic, details, or conclusion ___ Paragraph includes less than two research-based detail sentences ___ Research is not paraphrased in students' own words	
Creates Assessment Quiz Directly Aligned to Research	___ Students write more than five assessment questions related to the topic ___ Students include questions form four or more different levels of Bloom's Taxonomy	___ Students write at least five assessment questions related to the topic ___ Students include questions from at least three different levels of Bloom's Taxonomy ___ Students include an answer key with correct answers	___ Students write at least four assessment questions related to the topic ___ Students include questions from at least two different levels of Bloom's Taxonomy ___ Students include an answer key with some correct answers	___ Students write less than four assessment questions related to the topic ___ Students include questions from less than two different levels of Bloom's Taxonomy ___ Students do not include an answer key or most answers are incorrect	

Having the rubric ahead of time allows the students to design their output around clear outcomes that they will need to demonstrate. There won't be surprises for the students, or arbitrary grading.

Students are then allowed to work together in pairs to complete the assignment. Two students turn in the product shown in Figure 4.4.

Figure 4.4. Student Product

The Whale

By Austin and Noah

Whales are really big animals that live in the ocean. They eat krill, fish, and squid. They travel far distances to find their food. These long trips are called *migrations*. Whales migrate more than 5,000 miles to find their food! Whales are not fish. They are mammals because they have to breathe air. They use their blowholes to breathe. Whales can be bigger than the dinosaurs were! They have a layer of *blubber* under their skin. Blubber keeps them warm. Only sharks and people kill whales because they are so big.

1. What do whales eat?
   A. Other whales
   B. Squid
   C. Humans

2. Whales are…
   A. People
   B. Mammals
   C. Neither

3. How do whales breathe?
   A. They use their blowholes
   B. They take the air from people
   C. Whales don't breathe

4. Can whales be bigger than dinosaurs?
   A. No
   B. Yes
   C. Maybe

5. Why do whales have blubber?
   A. It's just there
   B. To keep them warm
   C. To make them cold

6. What kills whales?
   A. Sharks
   B. People
   C. Both

Using the rubric, the teacher conveys the feedback shown in Figure 4.5 to the students.

Figure 4.5. Teacher Feedback Using Rubric

	Performance Level				Score (1–4)
	Advanced 4	Proficient 3	Basic 2	Below 1	
Composes Research-Based Paragraph about a Mammal	___ Students write multiple paragraphs _X_ Paragraph includes more than three research-based detail sentences	___ Paragraph is complete with topic, details, & conclusion _X_ Paragraph includes at least three research-based detail sentences _X_ All research is paraphrased in students' own words	_X_ Paragraph is missing either the topic, details, or conclusion ___ Paragraph includes at least two research-based detail sentences ___ Some research is paraphrased in students' own words	___ Paragraph is missing majority of topic, details, or conclusion ___ Paragraph includes less than two research-based detail sentences ___ Research is not paraphrased in students' own words	2
Creates Assessment Quiz Directly Aligned to Research	_X_ Students write more than five assessment questions related to the topic ___ Students include questions from four or more different levels of Bloom's Taxonomy	_X_ Students write at least five assessment questions related to the topic ___ Students include questions from at least three different levels of Bloom's Taxonomy ___ Students include an answer key with correct answers	___ Students write at least four assessment questions related to the topic _X_ Students include questions from at least two different levels of Bloom's Taxonomy ___ Students include an answer key with some correct answers	___ Students write less than four assessment questions related to the topic ___ Students include questions from less than two different levels of Bloom's Taxonomy _X_ Students do not include an answer key or most answers are incorrect	2
					4/8

The students wrote a solid paragraph, but did not close the writing with a proper conclusion.

- The students wrote more than the required amount of detailed sentences, with enough information to expand the paragraph into two or three paragraphs.

- From the rubric feedback, the students also learn that, although they went above and beyond in the quantity of the questions they wrote, they did not meet the goal for the variety in questions that they needed.

- The two students failed to turn in an answer key.

Now Mrs. Johnson will conference with these students, reviewing their rubric to determine the needs of the students and her next steps for instruction

- Because the lack of a conclusion sentence was the result of an obvious oversight by capable students, Mrs. Johnson simply reminds the students to edit their work before turning in an assignment. Had this not been the case, she would have devised a mini-lesson to reteach the components of a good paragraph, emphasizing the conclusion.

- Only after the students mastered the concept of concluding a single paragraph, could the teacher and students move into a three-paragraph essay model consisting of topic, supporting, and concluding paragraphs. Mrs. Johnson sets this as the next step for these two students as they have demonstrated that they are ready to move to this level.

- Additionally, Mrs. Johnson learns that the majority of her students had difficulty with creating questions at various levels of Bloom's Taxonomy. Although they can aptly answer all types of questions during reading, she needs to continue to work with her class to allow them more time to learn how to generate such questions.

- As a final point, the two students failed to turn in an answer key for this assignment. Mrs. Johnson reminds them that to receive a proficient grade, they must provide the answers to the questions that they create. Rather than have them answer the existing questions, Mrs. Johnson allows the students to submit only the answers for the reconstructed sentences that they will write.

Mrs. Johnson then conferences with the other students in the class providing individual, timely feedback specific to the rubric descriptors. Depending on the output of the other students in the class, she designs differentiated lessons to reinforce skills either individually, through small group instruction, or as entire class lessons. She gives them the chance to go back and allow for multiple opportunities to reach proficiency in all areas based on the feedback they received.

This practice is supported and strongly encouraged by Robert Marzano (2006) when he quotes the following statement from John Hattie: "The most powerful single modification that enhances student achievement is feedback" (p. 96). Although this is a time-consuming process in the beginning, students eventually learn to work mostly from the rubric feedback, only clarifying questions with the teacher. To reduce the teacher's input even more, Marzano advocates enabling students to participate in the feedback process, stating that doing so also produces many gainful effects. So why not allow students to fill out their own rubrics when they are adequately prepared?

In all cases, rubrics can provide much more information to teachers and students than a mere percentage score on a test. Rubrics are a helpful tool in assessing as we go to gain data about what students know and are able to do. Rubrics help us as assessment pieces and are excellent teaching tools. You can teach your students what the rubric looks like and what each benchmark on the rubric means. This gives students a clearly defined objective, or target for performance. Rubrics serve a dual role. We're assessing as we go and using what we are doing in our classrooms to gain data about what students know.

Goal Tracking Sheets

Another helpful way to collect data of student learning is by using *goal tracking sheets.* Goal tracking sheets are useful because they document the progress of the students as the students work. They establish patterns and record strengths and weaknesses. At first inspection, goal-tracking sheets may look similar to general checklists or anecdotal notes that were once commonly, and sometimes still, used in classrooms. The main difference is that unlike the checklists and notes, these tools always need to be specific to a learning goal.

Consider, for example, a teacher who must collect and report data to parents on whether or not students listen critically and respond appropriately. Although this is a skill that the teacher must monitor and assess, it is not easily assessed through a test format. In addition, one isolated opportunity would not provide an adequate picture of student ability. Therefore, using a checklist to gather information over time would allot students multiple opportunities for practice and give the teacher a more comprehensive look at student achievement of this goal.

Each time the teacher engages in an activity that lends itself to students listening and responding, the teacher can pull out this checklist and record data along with the lesson. For instance, the class can read a selection in their language arts book and the teacher may stop along the way to discuss and ask questions about the content. This would be an advantageous time to record students' performance toward the anticipated goal of listening critically and responding appropriately. Another day, students might be asked to listen to classmates present oral reports in social studies and prepare questions to ask at the end of each presentation. Again the teacher could use this activity to assess student ability to meet this objective.

As shown in Figure 4.6, the goal is specifically listed as the title or heading. The names of the students are listed along the side, and dates are listed across the top. The dates represent each time the teacher does an activity or an assignment that would assess listening critically and responding appropriately. To track assessments more specifically, the teacher could also include a title or a descriptor of the assignment as a reminder when looking back over time. A general grading key is included to indicate advanced, proficient, basic, or below status. The teacher (or team) would develop exact descriptors of what each would look like at a specific grade level based on grade-level expectations or standards.

Figure 4.6. Goal Tracking Sheet—Example 1

Goal Tracking Sheet

Listening and Speaking: Listens critically and responds appropriately

Name	Date										
	11/20/07	11/29/07	12/13/07	12/21/07	1/9/08	1/17/08	1/29/08				
Taylor	4	4	3	4	4	4	4				
Noah	1	2	1	2	2	Ab	2				
Connor	2	2	2	3	3	2	3				
Christopher	3	3	Ab	2	Ab	3	3				
Colin	1	2	3	1	2	2	2				

KEY: 4: Advanced/Independent 3: Proficient/Instructional 2:Basic/Developing 1: Below Basic/Beginning

Looking at the dates, a teacher can determine if students are receiving adequate practice. Dates should be spread out over time to provide opportunities in between assessments for students to practice and improve their skills. Examining a collection of student grades can then paint the picture of student achievement. Using this data, teachers can assess needs for specific students, determine benchmark steps for those not meeting the goal, and provide differentiated instruction to help each student reach proficiency.

Using this type of goal tracking sheet as a way of collecting data is merely a way of establishing a pattern indicative of student ability. It is not intended that grades are added up and averaged at the end of each reporting period. Let's look back at the sample sheet in Figure 4.6 to better illustrate this idea.

Taylor, for example, consistently demonstrates ability above and beyond grade-level expectations. Although there was one day in December when she received only a proficient grade, she should not be penalized for one isolated assignment. Perhaps Taylor did not feel well that day. Maybe she was not interested in the content of the lesson. Or possibly she didn't understand the way the question was posed. Whatever the reason, Taylor has since demonstrated a solid pattern of being able to exceed the grade-level standard for that goal and that is what should be reported.

Noah has established a pattern as well. In looking at his grades, it is clear that Noah had difficulty with this concept when it was first introduced. If the teacher was working with Noah to improve those skills, it is not surprising that he began to improve, showing a pattern of developing this skill. Although Noah was absent for one of the assessment opportunities, he is not required to make it up, nor does he receive a grade of zero for this missed opportunity. If Noah's grades were averaged together (including his zero), he would receive a grade of 1.43, indicative of a student working below basic rather than the basic pattern he has sustained for three assessments over a month's time.

Other students, such as Connor and Colin, may need more opportunities to demonstrate a solid pattern of ability. For Connor, it appears that he is proficient in the skill, however, he is still not consistent on each assessment. Colin has established a pattern, but his inconsistent grades in the beginning would indicate that the teacher may want to work more closely with him to ensure that he understood the expectation of the goal and what he needed to do to demonstrate an aptitude for that skill. Students may also have special circumstances contributing to their learning such as being an English learner or perhaps receiving special education services for a learning disability. Whatever the case, the teacher would continue to assess until it was clear what each student could do at any given point in time.

Figure 4.7 (page 48) illustrates another type of goal-tracking sheet. At first glance, this type of goal tracking might remind educators of a simple way of collecting anecdotal notes. And it is. However, the *purpose* for collecting is quite different. With anecdotal notes, we tend to collect random data of what we see, such as "*Julio was tapping his pencil*" or "*Mollie worked slowly and was unable to complete the assignment.*" Sometimes anecdotal notes are used to track behavior over a period of time, looking for trends in that behavior. However, the distinction between anecdotal notes and goal-tracking sheets is that goal-tracking sheets are always tied to a specific learning goal.

Figure 4.7. Goal Tracking Sheet—Example 2

Learning Goal: Writes a descriptive paragraph with topic sentence, supporting sentences, and conclusion sentence.

Name: *Jermaine*		Name: *Mollie*	
Strengths	**Next Steps**	**Strengths**	**Next Steps**
Format *Uses descriptive language*	*Sentence variation*	*Capitalization* *Punctuation*	*Transition words*
Name: *Amy*		Name: *Julio*	
Strengths	**Next Steps**	**Strengths**	**Next Steps**
Topic sentence *Conclusion*	*Supporting details*	*Descriptive sentences* *Spelling*	*Add in high-level vocabulary*
Name: *Chris*		Name:	
Strengths	**Next Steps**	**Strengths**	**Next Steps**
Well-developed paragraph *High-level vocabulary*	*Multiple paragraphs*		
Name:		Name:	
Strengths	**Next Steps**	**Strengths**	**Next Steps**

Like the checklist format for goal tracking, the goal or the benchmark is clearly stated at the top. Although more time-consuming to fill out than a checklist, this format, allows for more detail in what the student can do and what the next steps for instruction should be. In this specific example, the teacher chose to use descriptive paragraph writing as a learning goal. Instead of spending hours grading every paragraph with a rubric, the teacher can simply use this form as a way to collect data and provide specific, timely feedback to students. By scanning each student's paper, the teacher can find obvious strengths and an overarching sense of an appropriate next step for each student. In addition, this could be done while the students are writing. The teacher would circulate around the room, observe students as they work, and provide immediate feedback to students about their progress.

Even though the entire class is working on the same goal, it is clear to see how the teacher is differentiating for each student. Amy is still concentrating on generating supporting sentences, whereas Chris is ready to expand his writing into multiple paragraphs. By recording the data on the goal-tracking sheet, both the teacher and students know where to focus when provided the next opportunity for practice. Furthermore, this data collection serves as a way of developing the assessment picture over time rather than a grade from one essay at the end of the trimester.

Verification Logs

Data demonstrating student learning can also be collected using a tool we call *verification logs*. Use of verification logs is a way to track work over time, allow for teacher communication and feedback, clarify troublesome topics, and provide skill practice. Initially, we believed that one could do these things in a journal. However, we prefer the terminology of verification log (opposed to journal) to ensure the distinction between the two. Although a journal is a place to practice skills, a verification log is a tool to practice, assess, and improve skills and demonstrate knowledge. A verification log could be a small notebook of continuous learning, or a three-ring binder that can be sectioned off and added to.

We would venture to guess that this tool is widely underused in classrooms today. The usual journals used in schools are writing journals—the teacher distributes them and the students write. Often times they are not collected or graded, and little feedback is given to the students for the amount of time and effort they have invested. As a result, students continue to produce the same output time after time.

But just imagine the possibilities. Making the switch from *traditional* journal use, teachers can utilize verification logs across content areas to give students the same chance to practice skills while receiving assessment feedback. Let's use science as an example. A student could use a verification log to demonstrate understanding of a concept or to record observations. Teachers could ask students to write down each step of an experiment to verify that the student understands the process, not just the final answer. They could write predictions before engaging in learning and justify their conclusions with learning from their textbooks. Teachers could use these logs as a way to verify what the student knows and is able to do without resorting to yet another test.

Also, consider social studies. In middle school, students often study about the *Great Age of Discovery*. A verification log could easily be used to check for understanding and compile a record of learning over time. For instance, a teacher might assign students to use their verification log to create a map to illustrate the great voyages of discovery and the locations of the routes. After the student created the map and labeled the routes, the teacher would provide a written response to the student's output (Figure 4.8).

Figure 4.8. Verification Log for the Great Age of Discovery

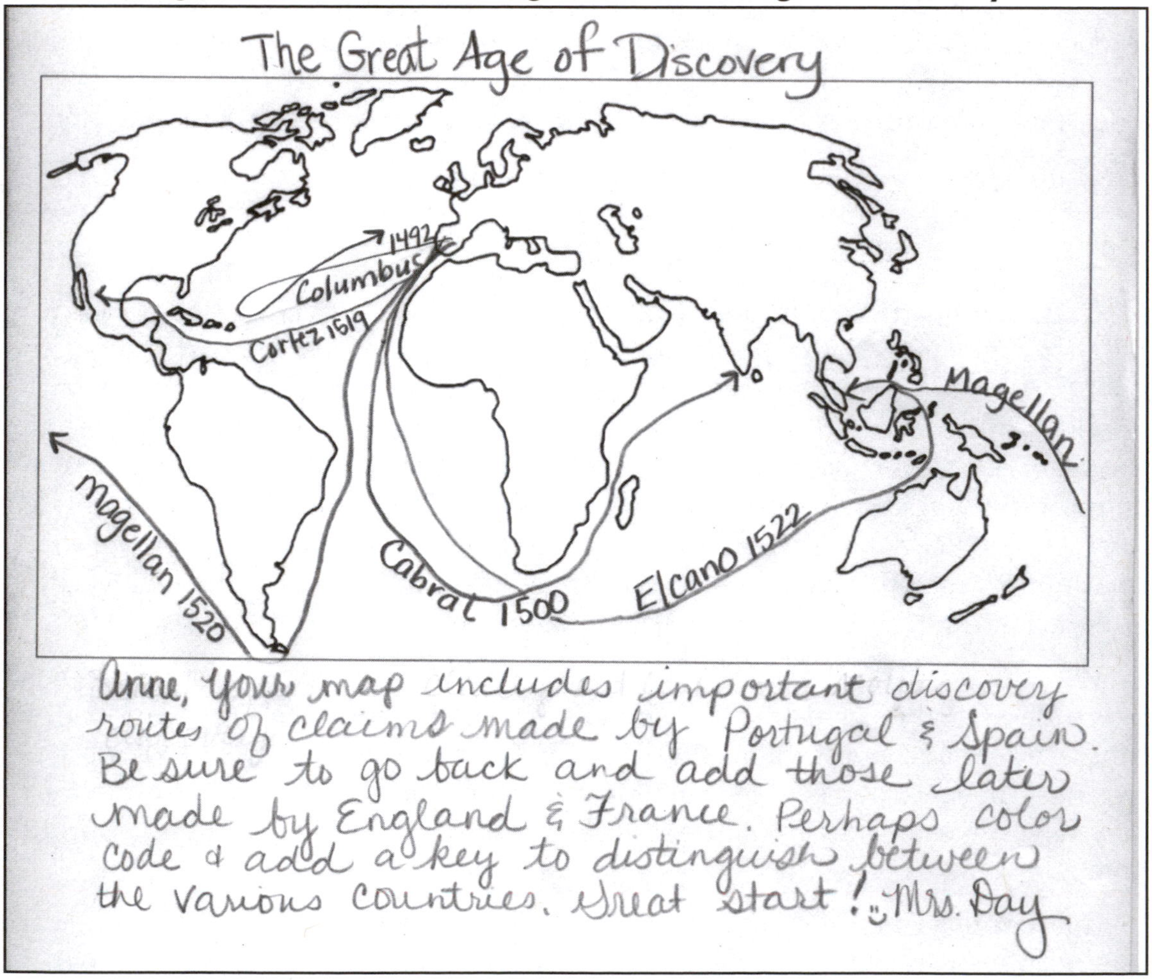

In this example, the teacher has provided individual feedback to the student to extend learning and provide the student with another opportunity to demonstrate the intended learning goal. The teacher could continue to use this log to assess the student's abilities to analyze political and economic change in the *Age of Exploration, the Age of Enlightenment,* and the *Age of Reason.* Subsequent verification log assignments might be to design and complete a chart indicating the exchanges of plants, animals, technology, culture, and ideas among Europe, Africa, Asia, and the Americas in the fifteenth and sixteenth centuries, and include economic and social effects on each continent. Or, using a Venn Diagram, discuss how the principles in the *Magna Carta* were embodied in such documents as the English *Bill of Rights* and the American *Declaration of Independence.*

Verification logs can also be used in math. In math, students can use verification logs to reflect on their understanding of concepts being taught. A student might be asked to reflect on what they know about the distributive process and give an example. Or they may write the steps to dividing fractions to verify that they understand what they are doing as opposed to the rote repetition of the algorithm. Often times we see students memorizing "tricks" to help them solve complex problems. For instance, we have seen teachers use catchy phrases such as "My Dear Aunt Sally" to remember the order of operations, and "leave me alone, change my name, turn me upside down" for division of fractions.

In the latter, a student asked to solve the following equation,

$$\tfrac{1}{2} \div \tfrac{1}{4} = ?$$

would leave ½ the same, change division to multiplication, and invert the ¼ to 4. After multiplying, the student would have accurately solved the problem, but most likely have no concept of what happened to the number they just divided. With verification logs, teachers can assess the level of student understanding and then respond in the log to help the student move to the next level. The response of the teacher then becomes a reference tool that the student can go back to review at any time.

Consider also using verification logs for vocabulary. Instead of a running record of definitions copied from the dictionary, students can use verification logs to demonstrate understanding of the words as well. Kate Kinsella and Kevin Feldman, renowned staff developers in vocabulary instruction, outline this format succinctly. They explain that the problem with dictionary definitions is that they do not explain; they define. Instead, teachers should provide the student with the word and the appropriate definition to be learned. The student demonstrates understanding by providing examples and a student-friendly definition. The teacher can assess understanding by asking quick yes/no questions that would verify whether or not the student had a solid understanding of the word.

Of course, a teacher would not use a verification log format when introducing new words. Good instruction dictates that the students be provided time to learn and practice the words through structured, scaffolded activities and discussions. Once the teacher felt the students had received ample instruction and practice with the vocabulary, an assessment would be given. A verification log would take the place of a traditional test and give a more complex view of student understanding. Figure 4.9 (page 53) encompasses the ideas of Kate Kinsella and Kevin Feldman of what a page in a vocabulary verification log might look like.

The teacher might choose to complete the example column through guided practice and have the students complete the frame column independently. The teacher would also provide the assessment questions that the students would be required to answer. The teacher would use the completed log to assess the understanding of her students and would differentiate the level of support based on the skill level of each student.

Figure 4.9. Vocabulary Verification Log

Word and Definition	Examples	Student Definition/Frame	Assess (Yes/No)
beloved adj. & n. dearly loved a person who is dearly loved	◆ My husband and son/family ◆ Photographs/ memories ◆ Mrs. Wing/friend	_____ is/ are my beloved _____.	Could you have a beloved…? ◆ injury ◆ Game Boy ◆ mom ◆ enemy ◆ dog ◆ punishment
claim(ed) v. to demand as one's own or one's right	◆ The explorers claimed Indian land as their own. ◆ I claimed the front seat of the car by yelling "Shotgun!"	I claimed _____ was mine.	Will you claim…? ◆ a million $ ◆ to be the one who smells bad ◆ the last ice cream ◆ a lost bracelet ◆ to be a Barney fan
brutal adj. savagely cruel	◆ 9-11 was a brutal attack on the United States. ◆ Cancer is a brutal illness that kills millions each year. ◆ I moved to San Diego because of the brutal winters back east. ◆ The brutal effects of Hurricane Katrina were devastating.	I think _____ is/was brutal.	Would you consider the following to be brutal? ◆ a shot at the doctors ◆ going to bed without dessert ◆ an ice cream party ◆ losing your Game Boy as a punishment ◆ a trip to Soak City ◆ the war in Iraq ◆ being lost at sea
transform(ed) v. to change greatly in appearance or form	◆ caterpillar to butterfly ◆ princess and warrior to volcano ◆ tadpole to frog	_____ transformed into _____.	Would you call these things transformed? ◆ writing going from one paragraph to five ◆ brushing your hair ◆ growing up (kid to adult) ◆ brushing your teeth

Exit Slips and Checklists

Exit slips and checklists are probably the most convenient way to assess as you go. These tools help assess student understanding of new or old concepts, determine where students need additional clarification or assistance, and require students to restate learning in their own words. Although commonly used, we must again remind teachers that to use these tools effectively, they must be tied to learning goals.

Exit slips are a quick way to check for understanding. Of course, these exit slips would not be extremely helpful in determining report card grades, but they can certainly help teachers inform instruction. A quick sort of the slips would indicate who understood the objective and who didn't, if the teacher needed to re-teach to the class, if a small group mini lesson was needed, or if she were ready to move on in her instruction. For example, if the learning goal is for students to be able to describe the setting using at least three details (adapting the work of Rick Stiggins), an effective exit slip might look like the one in Figure 4.10.

Figure 4.10. Exit Slip

Exit Slip

Name: _____   Date:_____

Learning Goal: *Students can identify the setting of a story*

Three details I remember about the setting of the story are:

1.

2.

3.

When implementing exit slips, each student is required to fill one out and hand it to the teacher when "exiting" the class. Using transition time for this activity reduces down time and maximizes instructional time. The teacher stands in the doorway to ensure that every student is accountable for turning in a slip. After the students leave, the teacher separates the slips into clearly defined evidence of who understands and who doesn't. Students with three accurate details are placed in one pile, those with one to two acceptable details in another, and those without details or incorrect details in a third pile. For example, if a student provided details describing the characters, it would not show an understanding of the setting.

Depending on how many slips are in each pile, the teacher would know whether it was appropriate to speed up or slow down instruction.

Take the exit slip concept and apply it at a more advanced level such as seventh or eighth grade, and it essentially works the same way. For example, eighth grade students might be asked to analyze idioms, analogies, metaphors, and similes to infer the literal and figurative meanings of phrases. In the exit slip format, it would look something like Figure 4.11.

Figure 4.11. Exit Slip

Exit Slip
Name: _____ Date:_____
Learning Goal: *Students can analyze idioms, analogies, metaphors, and similes to infer the literal and figurative meanings of phrases.*
Choose an answer to the following analogy.
JUDGE : IMPARTIAL ::   (A) animal : tame   (B) acrobat : limber   (C) dignitary : proud   (D) prisoner : repentant   (E) politician : liberal
Demonstration of Understanding: *Justify your answer.*

Exit slips do not have to be actual slips, but could also be a poll of students as they leave the class or return to their seats. For instance, in a class of vocabulary development for English learners, a teacher can ask students to tell her a word (or use a word) that they remember from the lesson. Using a checklist, the teacher would mark if the student used a basic-level or a high-level word. She can then decide if she needs to emphasize the lesson vocabulary again with the entire class or just individual students. Furthermore, tracking the level of words over time would help the teacher identify which students needed more vocabulary development, and which students were ready to apply words at a more advanced level.

Figure 4.12 depicts a basic checklist of "exit polls" that a teacher could create to track student responses.

Figure 4.12. Exit Poll

Vocabulary Development—2nd Grade

	Chinatown 9/15		The Rainbow Fish 9/31		Stellaluna 10/5	
	Basic	*High*	*Basic*	*High*	*Basic*	*High*
Rachel	√		√		√	
Gregorio		√		√		√
Mayra	√			√		√
Isabel		√		√		√
Nazat	√		√		√	

By merely glancing at the chart, the teacher can see that she will need to work closely with Rachel and Nazat to help them acquire higher-level vocabulary. Mayra seems to be coming along, and Isabel and Gregorio are possibly ready to start using words in sentences and applying them to alternative contexts.

Knowing the words the students are choosing would give the teacher more specific information to design instruction around and serve as a reminder of what words to reinforce over time. Therefore, instead of using a check in each column, the teacher could quickly jot down the word as in Figure 4.13.

Figure 4.13. Alternative Exit Poll

Vocabulary Development—2nd Grade

	Chinatown 9/15		The Rainbow Fish 9/31		Stellaluna 10/5	
	Basic	*High*	*Basic*	*High*	*Basic*	*High*
Rachel	apartment		shiny		branch	
Gregorio		cobbler		scales		limb
Mayra	street			glittering		survive
Isabel		Tai-Chi		scales		behave
Nazat	street		fish		bat	

Again, this all happens after teaching has occurred when the teacher wants to determine what the students have learned from that instruction. Gathering this type of assessment information is as easy as deciding on a goal, creating a simple chart to collect the data, standing by the door, and recording responses as students leave for recess. Using this three-minute process, teachers will obtain immediate data as well as progress data over time if repeated periodically.

Now let us consider Mr. Henry. Mr. Henry is a third grade teacher with a goal that all of his students will memorize single-digit multiplication facts 0 to 12. Each week he is introducing a new fact base. After practice in class, he gives students a daily quiz of fifty problems. He has twenty students in his class, and at the end of the week, he has 100 papers to correct (5,000 problems)! He corrects the papers over the weekend, and records the grades in his grade book. On Monday he must move on to the next fact base to keep up with his pacing guide. He continues this routine for twelve weeks until he has taught all of the required facts. At the end, he gives a cumulative test, and 75% of his class scores below standard. Mr. Henry would like to use the remaining six weeks of the trimester to reteach, review, and provide small-group instruction, but he must move on to division to ensure he covers his required content before report cards are due.

Mr. Henry is understandably overwhelmed with the amount of papers he is correcting to track students' mastery of multiplication facts. In addition, the quiz data he is collecting is not timely, nor does it help inform his instruction. With so many of his students not succeeding, Mr. Henry knows he must try something different.

The school principal suggests that Mr. Henry try using a checklist method for collecting the same information. Together they devise a simple system where Mr. Henry will ask each student one fact at the end of every lesson by randomly pulling sticks with each student's name. The students will have three seconds to respond with the correct answer at which time Mr. Henry will record a simple yes or no ($\sqrt{}$/−) on his checklist. Allotting ten seconds per student (to present the problem, wait for a response, and record the outcome) will amount to a total of just over three minutes of his instructional time. Figure 4.14 (page 58) outlines the data that Mr. Henry collected in November. Although each student only answers one fact, using the checklist often for the same skill will provide a pattern over time that will eliminate the suggestion of a "lucky guess."

At the end of each week, Mr. Henry looks for a trend that the majority (85%) of his class is demonstrating proficiency on that factor. For 3-based facts, he concludes that he is ready to move on, however a few students need some extra practice. Therefore, the next week he moves on to 4-based facts, but modifies his instructional block. He teaches the new information to the entire class, but when the students begin their independent practice, he calls Sharyn, Jimmy, and Shaun for a small group. He again reviews 3-based facts, but this time he uses manipulatives to further illustrate the conceptual understanding. By Tuesday, he affirms that Shaun does not need the small-group instruction, but continues to provide structured guided practice to Sharyn and Jimmy of both 3- and 4-based facts.

Figure 4.14. Math Checklist

Multiplication Facts—3rd Grade
November

	Factor 3					Factor 4					Factor 5					Factor 6									
	3x	3x	3x	3x	3x	4x	4x	4x	4x	4x	5x	5x	5x	5x	5x	6x	6x	6x	6x	6x	6x	6x	6x	6x	6x
Billy	✓	✓	✓	✓	✓	✓	✓	✓	✓	✓	✓	✓	✓	✓	✓	✓	✓	✓	✓	✓	✓	✓	✓	✓	✓
Paul	✓	✓	✓	✓	✓	—	—	✓	✓	✓	✓	✓	✓	—	✓	—	—	—	—	—	—	✓	✓	✓	✓
Sharyn	—	—	✓	—	✓	—	—	✓	✓	—	—	—	✓	—	✓	—	—	✓	—	—	—	—	—	—	—
Dan	✓	✓	✓	✓	✓	✓	✓	—	✓	✓	✓	✓	✓	✓	✓	✓	—	—	✓	—	✓	✓	—	✓	—
Kim	✓	✓	✓	✓	✓	—	—	—	✓	✓	✓	✓	✓	✓	✓	—	—	—	—	—	—	—	—	—	—
Jimmy	—	—	✓	—	✓	—	—	✓	✓	✓	✓	✓	✓	✓	✓	—	✓	—	—	✓	✓	—	✓	✓	✓
Shaun	—	—	✓	✓	✓	✓	✓	✓	✓	✓	✓	✓	✓	✓	✓	✓	—	✓	✓	—	—	✓	✓	✓	✓
David	✓	—	✓	✓	✓	✓	✓	—	✓	—	✓	✓	✓	✓	✓	✓	✓	✓	✓	✓	—	✓	✓	✓	✓
Kathy	✓	✓	✓	✓	✓	✓	✓	✓	✓	✓	✓	✓	✓	✓	✓	—	✓	✓	—	✓	—	✓	✓	✓	✓
Rose	✓	✓	✓	✓	✓	✓	✓	✓	✓	✓	✓	✓	✓	✓	✓	—	✓	—	—	✓	✓	✓	✓	✓	✓

At the end of week two, he again decides that he is ready to move his class ahead. He continues to work independently with Sharyn, who is still struggling, and enlists the help of a peer tutor to provide her extra support during the day. He also notes that he will need to check in with Kim, Jimmy, and Paul to ensure that they indeed are on track with their facts. He then teaches 5-based facts, and after only a few days, he deduces that the class has memorized the rule. Although the pacing guide delineates that he stay on the five tables for another two days, Mr. Henry decides to use this gift of time to move on to 6-based facts.

From the data, Mr. Henry sees that he has made a good choice. The six tables prove to be difficult for a large portion of his class, and so he resolves to slow down and spend more time with all students. Billy and Kathy, however, seem to have no difficulty. So instead of pulling a small review group this week, Mr. Henry pulls an extension group. Billy and Kathy work with Mr. Henry to apply their understanding to mathematical puzzles and word problems to further expand their understanding. During the next week Rose, David, and Shaun join the enrichment group as they demonstrate competency of the skill. Now Shaun, who could have been tracked into extra support for many weeks, has moved from extra support to enrichment groups all within the same month.

Mr. Henry is pleased with his new system of assessment. He is able to gather quick data to track student progress. He is using the data to inform his instruction and modifying his pacing to accommodate and differentiate for the needs of his students. He has made time for small-group and individual instruction, and he has data that tells him who should be in each session. But the best part for Mr. Henry is that he has no papers to grade and record on the weekend!

Well, not as many papers. Mr. Henry decides that he still wants to give his students paper and pencil quiz practice of their multiplication facts. However, instead of fifty practice problems of the same fact each day, he provides a mixed review practice every few weeks covering all of the facts studied to that point. This data along with his daily data will provide him with a more comprehensive picture of the ability of his students. It will also give him an idea of how well his students are retaining the information before he finds out differently twelve weeks too late.

Again, exit slips and checklists will not provide teachers with grades to record or pinpoint exact difficulties that students are experiencing. However, they can help reduce the amount of quizzes and tests that we give to students and paint a relatively accurate assessment picture. Exit slips and checklists can be utilized as instruction occurs, having a greater impact on student learning. Teachers can then use the data collected to plan lessons and modify instruction.

Summary

Because the focus of this book is on reducing the layers of assessment, it's important that we understand that there is absolutely a place and time for summative assessment. We are not completely eliminating formal assessment, but we are providing alternative ways to gather data. Analyzing and applying data is no easy task. Therefore, we must remain clear on our approach and keep it simple enough so that it actually happens.

Schools will still want to set overarching goals which need to be revisited periodically at staff meetings. Rather than bringing a grade sheet with percentages and averages for a class, teachers could instead be asked to implement and bring verification logs. Verification logs are an easy way to spark conversation about student progress. They also provide a clear picture of what a teacher is doing to ensure student success, confirm alignment to standards or previously set expectations, and allow time to examine rigor of assignments. Remember Bob in Chapter 2. This would be a way for Bob to record evidence on school goals without losing sight of his individual classroom goals.

Team goals, set at team meetings, also need to be monitored frequently and used to drive many of the collaborative conversations of these groups. For these meetings, teammates might choose to bring goal-tracking sheets or rubrics with work samples that indicate progression toward the common goals. Teams could discuss student growth, decide on future common assessments, and create ideas to extend, practice, or reteach necessary concepts.

Teachers also need to track their individual goals. For these goals, teachers could use exit slips and checklists. Using these tools, teachers could easily determine which areas to frequently assess and monitor. They could add these assessments to their lesson plans, enabling them to collect daily data on these goals.

These data-collection methods lend themselves to better collaboration with parents, students, and grade level teams. Again, remember Bob in Chapter 2. This new repertoire of assessment possibilities could provide him with a solution for effectively organizing and tracking his data. As a result, he would be better equipped to report feedback to students and parents, leading to true differentiation and improved instruction.

5

Recording Evidence

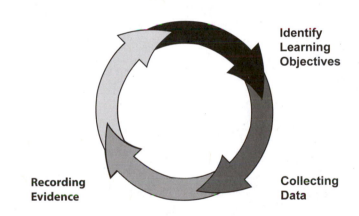

Identify
Learning
Objectives

Collecting
Data

Recording
Evidence

Even if we can help educators streamline effective ways to identify learning objectives and collect data, the process falls short without manageable ways to record the evidence of student learning. Consequently, the next step in the process after we've identified the learning objective and we've collected the data, is to find a way to record that data so as to give us the most accurate information about what the students know. We also need to decide how to monitor the student learning so as to guide our instruction.

In addition, we must discuss the assignment of grades to this evidence and we must agree on the purpose for assigning grades. Is the purpose of grading to communicate progress, or is it to inform our instruction? If the goal of grades is communication of student progress and current skills, do our grading practices reflect this? Likewise, what evidence do we have that justifies this judgment? If the purpose of grades is to inform our instruction, how do we use grades to serve this purpose? And, is it possible to record evidence in the hopes of doing both?

In a traditional grading system teachers use grade books to track test data and assignment grades. We list the grades for all of the class work, homework, projects and tests that have been given. There may or may not be an opportunity for "extra" credit. We also determine what to do on the occasion that a student was absent or did not turn in their work. We may assign a zero, or in some cases ignore it. Finally we assign weighted percentages to each grade indicating the importance of the assessment or assignment. Once we have all of our numbers recorded, we average the grades and record that average on the report card at the end of the term.

Using a spreadsheet program like Microsoft Excel, a grade book might look something like Figure 5.1.

Figure 5.1. An Excel-Style Grade Book

	A	B	C	D	E	F	G	H	I	J	K	L
1	**Name**	T1	T2	T3	P1	P2	H1	H2	H3	H4	Avg	Grade
2	Ann	89	78	100	88	92	100	95	78	88	89.6	
3	Bill	68	87	72	60	80	65	100	50	42		
4	Carol	98	87	100	78	99	80	100	88	95		
5	Doug	78	68	92	88	76	95	99	88	72		
6	Elaine	89	78	100	88	92	100	95	78	88		
7	Frank	79	69	97	95	82	99	93	75	78		
8	Gloria	98	87	100	78	99	80	100	88	95		
9	Howard	78	68	92	88	76	95	99	88	72		
10	Imogene	89	78	100	88	92	100	95	78	88		
11	John	89	78	100	88	92	100	95	78	88		
12	Kesha	79	69	97	95	82	99	93	75	78		
13												
14												
15												
16	T 1-3 = tests 1-3				Tests = 40%							
17	P 1-2 = projects 1-2				Projects = 50%							
18	H 1-4 = homework 1-4				Homework = 10%							
19												
20												

However, we suggest ditching this type of traditional grade book and replacing it with a variety of assessment feedback tools to record evidence of student progress. Assessment feedback should be a combination of all of the data that we have gathered throughout the course of the semester or year, not just a collection of numbers. By using the data from the things that we have discussed earlier, such as verification journals, rubric scores, and goal-tracking sheets in combination with the more traditional grade book where data for summative assessments has been recorded, grading becomes an exercise of our professional judgment as opposed to a mechanical numerical exercise (O'Connor, 2002). Our grades become a real reflection of the current level of knowledge that the students have as opposed to a snapshot in time on the day that the test was given or a reflection of a missed opportunity for learning.

Consider this grading experiment from Douglas Reeves (2008): "Calculate the final grade for a student who receives the following 10 grades during a semester: C, C, MA (Missing Assignment), D, C, B, MA, MA, B, A. Every time—bar none—you get the same results: The final grades range from F to A and include everything in between" (p. 85–87). This type of grading leads to inconsistent reporting of student knowledge and creates a very difficult situation in which to try to refine instruction to improve student success. When we are grading students it is critical that we have a clear understanding of what the grades mean and the next step to take as an effective instructor. "The most effective grading practices provide accurate, specific, timely feedback designed to improve student performance" (Reeves, 2008, p. 86).

We know that all kinds of learning—whether it is in the classroom, boardroom, or on an athletic field—requires effective feedback. However, the feedback that is given in schools isn't always effective. Jay McTighe and Ken O'Connor, in their article *Seven Practices for Effective Learning* (2005), tell us that to serve learning, feedback must meet four criteria: it must be timely, specific, understandable to the receiver, and formed to allow for self-adjustment. Therefore, if we are truly going to use grades as feedback, then we need to go back to the idea of identifying a clear understanding of the learning goal.

By looking at the objectives and identifying concrete benchmarks for mastery, we can begin to measure these objectives in very concrete ways. For example, if at the end of the year, a kindergartner needs to have mastered eight concepts of print and we have given this student multiple opportunities for success throughout the year, we can clearly define whether or not the student is able to perform this skill on a regular basis as opposed to the traditional system of sitting down with the student and giving the student a test on one day and recording a percentage of the number correct.

Figure 5.2 demonstrates how a teacher could record this data.

Figure 5.2. A Tool to Record Data

Kindergarten Reading Benchmark Tracking

Subject: _Reading_   Student Name: _Samad_   Trimester: _1_

Learning Objectives	Benchmark	Date					
		8/31/07	9/15/07	9/28/07	10/10/07		
Identifies Concepts About Print	8	2		8			
Rhymes Simple Words	7	0	Ab.		4		
Blends Sounds Into Words	7		Ab.	3	4		
Segments Words Into Sounds	7		Ab.	0	1		
Identifies Upper Case Letters	26	10	24	26			
Identifies Lower Case Letters	26	4	10		24		
Knows Letter Sounds	26	12		15	18		
Reads High Frequency Words	18		0		0		
Reading Level	AB						

In Figure 5.2, each of the benchmark assessments are scored to track progress toward the overall goal. If the goal is not met, the teacher continues to refine instruction and give the students multiple opportunities to show proficiency. Although these benchmark scores are not averaged, in districts still requiring traditional grading, they would play a large role in determining the report card grade. For example, in September this student is able to identify all capital letters. The teacher would therefore consider this student proficient in this area, and rather than average the bench mark scores of 10 out of 26 (38%), 24 out of 26 (92%), and 26 out of 26 (100%), and assigning a grade of a 76%. In addition, the teacher would look at other assessment measures to get a full picture of a student's skills before determining overall "grades."

Assessment feedback tools allow us to do just what they say: provide specific feedback regarding the level of knowledge that a student has at any given time throughout the school year. This concept continues to bring us back to the essential question that should be guiding our instruction. How do we know what students know and are able to do? And more importantly, what are we doing when they don't master the concepts being presented to them?

When setting up the assessment feedback tool (Figure 5.3) for recording evidence, start with your grade-level benchmarks and state standards. Identify the learning goals. Then record the proficiency for each of the standards for each assignment or assessment you are giving. Not only does this provide us with a clear picture of what students know, it acts as an instructional guide for us so that we can monitor our assignments to make sure that we have provided each student with enough opportunity to show mastery of the learning goal.

Using this tool, a teacher can track progress toward specific goals or standards. Notice that several of the assignments and assessments overlap in the goals that they address. A teacher using this tool to refine instruction would look for patterns in scores, and continue to refine instruction until proficiency is met. When using this same tool for grading purposes, the teacher would look at consistency of mastery. Later scores would be more reflective of current understanding and progress and therefore be more influential in the assignment of the grade.

More specifically, a teacher might look at the first indicator of goal #1: *Uses strategies to determine meaning of specialized vocabulary.* The student clearly demonstrates proficiency each time, so the implication for instruction is to provide ways to extend or enhance the learning for this student. The student was able to demonstrate advanced skills on the last assignment, but without evidence of consistency, the teacher would not be able to report advanced level skills at this time. For the second indicator of goal #1—*Reads narrative and expository text fluently*—the student showed signs of struggling at first. The records of these scores were an indication to the teacher to refine instruction to help develop the skill for this student. In the last three assessments, the student was clearly proficient in the skill. This would be the grade reported, not an average of the grades over time.

Figure 5.3. Assessment Feedback Tool

5th Grade LA/Social Studies/Science

Name: _____ **Student Learning Goals Key Standards Report Card Descriptors**	Assignment/Assessment												
	Assignment	Assessment	Assessment	Assignment	Assignment	Assessment	Assignment	Assignment	Assignment	Assessment	Assignment	Assessment	
Reading													
I. Uses strategies to determine meaning of specialized vocabulary	3				3					3	4		
Reads narrative and expository text with fluency		2	2			3		3				3	
II. Comprehends and analyzes informational text			2						2				
III. Comprehends and analyzes literature	3	2				2		3					
Reading effort	4			4	4		3	4		3	4		

4: Advanced   3: Proficient   2: Basic   1: Below Basic

With goals having limited scores, teachers would see that they would need to look at alternative ways to gather assessment data to create a more complete picture of student understanding. When scores are inconsistent, it would raise awareness for teachers to look closely at that area for the student to determine why the inconsistency. Likewise, effort is recorded as it's own grade to determine if students are working to their potential and to help keep grades specific to goals more objective.

The assessment feedback tool shown in Figure 5.3 is not the only way to assemble and record evidence of student learning. Another effective way to record evidence is by using evidence collections. Evidence collections are a modern spin on a traditional way of tracking student progress over time. They are powerful because they are authentic and evaluate the individual, not just the group. Evidence collections are organized, ongoing, and provide a descriptive picture of student learning that demonstrates the acquisition of skills as well as the application and construction of knowledge.

In looking at evidence collections, it is easy to mistake them for conventional student portfolios. However, unlike student portfolios that were often times random, evidence collections are systematic and directly aligned to goals. No longer can a child say "I got a 100% on my spelling test, so I am going to put it in my portfolio for my mother to see." Instead, the teacher decides, regardless of the grade, what goes in the evidence collection. In addition, all work collected is not simply filed under the student's name to be sorted at a later date. Folders labeled with specific goals are placed behind each child's name, and each assignment collected directly demonstrates that goal. Those teachers savvy enough to competently use technology might consider setting up web collections where students could post work to a folder that could be accessed both from home or at school.

Either way, it is this systematic approach that will provide insight into student progress based on goals being tracked.

Figure 5.4 clearly distinguishes between evidence collections and student portfolios.

Figure 5.4. Evidence Collections vs. Student Portfolios

Evidence Collections	Student Portfolios
◆ Systematic	◆ Random
◆ Aligned to goals	◆ Chosen by student
◆ Reviewed regularly to guide instruction	◆ Shared periodically to show student pride
◆ Provides opportunity for professional collaboration	◆ Does not get discussed with colleagues

Consider Bob from Chapter 2 again. If Bob needs to track progress toward school goals, grade level goals, and his individual classroom goals, an evidence collection would be an easy way for him to keep track of the three types of goals. When Bob goes to a staff or grade-level meeting, he would have information at his fingertips that shows what he is doing to work on each of the goals, and how his students are performing. If Bob finds an area to be limited in evidence, he would realize that his students need more opportunity to practice in that area. If his students are struggling, his colleagues could look at the assignments Bob is providing and offer suggestions for how to help his students improve. In addition, Bob would discover long before report card time where his students needed support, as opposed to finding out after the end of a trimester test when it is too late to do anything about it.

Yet, it is not only important for teachers to be reviewing the items in an evidence collection, students must also be a part of this process. After all, it will be the students who will need to know how to improve their work. As we discussed through the lens of rubrics, evidence collections are a great way for students to view their progress and be able to provide their own feedback on how they are doing. From that feedback, teachers can help guide students into creating their own differentiated goals. Unlike rubrics, however, evidence collections provide students and teachers a view over time as opposed to a view of a single event or activity.

It is helpful when having students review evidence collections to provide them with a reflection sheet to guide them toward their conclusions. The goal would be written at the top, and descriptors of what proficient would look like, or benchmark goals toward the main goal, would be generated as a reflection guide. This activity could be done even with very young students using smiley faces to indicate levels of achievement. Reflection sheets would vary in sophistication, depth of questions, and number of descriptors depending on the grade level and goal. For older students, you could use thumbs up, thumbs down, or thumb in the middle as graphics, or simple words such as yes, no, and partially achieved.

Consider the following reflection sheet (Figure 5.5, page 70) for emergent writers.

Figure 5.5. Reflection Sheet for Emergent Writers

Name: _____

Date: _____

Goal: Demonstration of Emergent Writing Skills

I can. . .			
Write my letters.			
Write the first sounds of words.			
Write with spaces between words.			
Read my writing.			
Write a simple sentence.			
Write with capitals and periods.			

A teacher could use a format like this to sit with a child to discuss writing samples from their evidence collection. The child would review their writing with guidance from the teacher and make judgments about their progress based on the descriptors on the reflection sheet. Then, goals would be generated and discussed through simple terminology and questioning such as, "What could we do to get a thumbs up for this statement?" or "You gave yourself an 'oh no' for not being able to read your writing. What could you do to improve that?"

The earlier we begin this process, the more critically students will learn to look at their work as they progress through school. Teachers limited on time could utilize parent volunteers or peer/cross-age tutors to help students complete this activity on a frequent basis. However, teachers would want to be sure to include themselves in this process and check in with all students regularly so that they know how each student is doing. Schools that make this process a part of their culture would benefit from grade to grade because students would be skillful at contributing to the monitoring of their own progress.

Summary

Unfortunately, using assessment feedback versus simply reporting grades is still cloudy territory for many schools. Guskey and Bailey (2001) provide us with the research-based rationale for why traditional practices need to change. Ken O'Connor (2002) shows us what an ideal system might look like. And still, almost a decade later, we still don't have a streamlined method in place to replace our antiquated system.

Educators need to come together to have conversations regarding grading practices. Weight of assessments, time of year, calibration of scores, and grading bias all need to be part of this discussion. Assessment tools are an essential part of the recording of evidence process. Figure 5.6 (page 72) outlines each assessment tool discussed in this book along with the purpose and recommendation for implementation for each.

Some schools are attempting to bridge old and new grading practices with sophisticated technological solutions. Many new electronic grading systems are popping up that propose easy solutions to recording grades. They allow for flexibility between percentage grading and rubric scores, they allow for a complete description of each assignment or assessment, they sort and record by standards, strands, and goals, and they even merge recorded grades to existing report cards! But do these tools truly reflect student learning and are teachers using them to modify instruction? In any case, it's a start.

Figure 5.6. Outline of Assessment Tools

Assessment Tool	Purpose	Recommendation for Implementation		
		CFU*	Refine	Report
Student Work Samples	Check that students can demonstrate understanding of concept being taught.	X	X	
Rubrics	Use as a checklist for progression of skills.		X	X
Goal Tracking Sheets	Check student understanding at any given point in time.	X	X	X
Verification Logs	Verify student understanding of skill.	X	X	
Checklists	Quick tracking of skill development.	X	X	
Exit Slips	Estimate student understanding of concept or skill.	X	X	
Evidence Collections	Track progress over time		X	X

*CFU—checking for understanding.

6

Refining Instruction

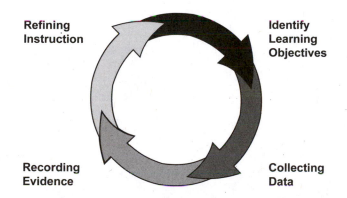

Refining
Instruction

Identify
Learning
Objectives

Recording
Evidence

Collecting
Data

This book has spent a good deal of time looking at assessment opportunities and the impact they have on student learning. But to achieve the desired levels of student learning, we must also consider instruction. It is imperative that professionals in the classroom constantly ask themselves what the next instructional steps are. These decisions must be based on the information that we are gathering from our students and through using the data of our daily practice. It is the final step in the assessment cycle that indicates whether we are ready to move on or whether we need to repeat the process.

In a traditional schooling system, time is our constant. School typically begins in September and ends in June. We know that parent conferences will be at the end of the first trimester and the state standardized testing happens in the spring. We only have a finite amount of time to "cover" our entire curriculum.

In this archaic system, learning becomes the variable by default. We cannot guarantee that all of our students will be ready to meet the benchmarks that the traditional system's calendar puts in front of them. Teachers feel bound by curriculum and pacing guides that keep moving forward even when students fall behind. And that is precisely what needs to change.

What we are able to guarantee is that all students can learn. To ensure learning for all students we need to find a way to create another shift in thinking, one in which learning is the constant and time is the variable. The following four action steps will help to clarify what this shift should look like. They outline a systematic process to begin the journey from "teaching to learning." Using this approach, we can provide multiple opportunities for success by continuously refining our instruction—but only if we prioritize, and only if we critically look at instructional refinement.

Action Step 1: Prioritize

As schooling becomes an increasingly complex system, we find ourselves faced with less and less time to cover everything that needs to be taught, let alone teach it! A wise life coach, Marilyn Tabor, once used this analogy:

> Imagine that you stop at the grocery store after work. You have twenty items on your list, but only enough time to pick up five of those items. Which items do you decide to buy?

Seeing academic concepts as items on a grocery list can help teachers prioritize the most essential concepts to teach. That doesn't mean that we don't go back to the grocery store at a later date to pick up the remaining items. However, we ensure that we buy the most essential items within the time frames we have.

Consider a team approach. Working together with other teachers can be akin to divvying up the shopping list. If one buys the items for appetizers, another for a main course, and a third for dessert, suddenly we are at a very successful progressive dinner. Teachers become skillful in the content and are not distracted by unfinished business in other content areas. They are able to focus on, teach, and refine the course they are assigned, like a chef perfecting a notable dish.

Now, refer back to identifying the learning objectives outlined in Chapter 3. It is here that we need to look at the objectives and identify the key standards being addressed. Doug Reeves (2008) explains key standards as being "essential knowledge and skills to move on to the next level…not an exhaustive list of standards that would be impossible to address in the time frame available" (p. 86). This identifies for us the importance of prioritizing the standards that are absolutely essential to the grade level or subject that we are teaching. When beginning the process of identifying key learning objectives teams should consider the following four criteria for each standard:

♦ *Endurance:* Will the standard provide students with knowledge and skills that will be of value beyond a single test date?

♦ *Leverage:* Will the standard provide knowledge and skills that will be of value in multiple disciplines?

♦ *Essential:* Will the standard provide essential knowledge and skills that are necessary for success in the next grade or level of instruction?

♦ *Assessable:* Does the standard have the ability to be measured?

The next step in prioritizing what we spend our time on is to identify the specific areas of need so as to refine our instruction. Refinement of instruction incorporates evaluating the success of demonstrating the intended learning outcome. It is critical that educators align their current reality to their desired results and set an appropriate course of action. It is at this stage of the game that we identify and use our available resources to impact the achievement of students. We need to set achievable, student centered and specific goals around the critical learning objectives as well as identify a plan of action so as to ensure that our students reach the target. If these goals are not achieved, we will need to try again. So what do we do with the other assignments and lessons we had planned? Simply put, we prioritize. Using the identified learning objectives as a guide, keep only those assignments that directly give you feedback on student learning of intended goals. Make all other assignments practice or extension opportunities. With this as an approach, teachers will find more time to reteach concepts to decreasing numbers of students. Remember that prioritizing is not akin to eliminating. The aforementioned process is a way to help teachers focus their time and energy on the key standards and the assignments and assessments directly aligned to those key standards in such a way that we can honestly say that learning is now our constant.

Finally, check the pacing of each lesson. Where can we speed up? What can we skip? Where do we need to slow down? Have we taken an honest look at our instructional practices? Are we teaching the keys concepts to mastery or have we merely covered the material? Teachers must not feel obliged to stick to a script or to teach a worksheet just because it is included in the curriculum. Many published curriculums include more material than humanely possible to teach. By remembering to use a pattern of continuous assessment, teachers will have the information they need about student learning to make informed decisions regarding the instruction that needs to occur each day. Teachers will be able to reduce the amount of items they are trying to handle and instead use the items they have in a more efficient way. Likewise, educators must also be willing to give up extraneous lessons taught traditionally every year. Again, this critical alignment to learning goals is one way we can refine instruction.

Action Step 2: Isolate the Breakdown and Target Instruction

Successful teachers discover the old adage that "'one size *doesn't* fit all" early on and quickly apply it to their instruction. For this reason it is important that we break the skill or concept that we are trying to teach into steps. Using state standards, grade-level benchmarks, and classroom assessments we can isolate the breakdown in our students' understanding and identify the discreet skills that are missing. For example, students must know their addition facts before they move on to subtraction. Letter names come before sounds and we teach the states before we expect students to learn the capitals. Although many lessons are taught to a collective whole, each student will come away from that instruction with a different level of understanding. Therefore, by varying the approach, a teacher can refine instruction specific to students' needs. For instance, some students learn best when taught individual steps that combine to create a complete process whereas others need to see the complete process in order to understand the discreet skills involved.

By conferencing with individual students, teachers can discover which approach might best serve the needs of the student and adjust their instruction accordingly. Conferences are also useful in pinpointing at what part of the instructional process the student's understanding broke down. Knowing this information, teachers can put scaffolds in place to support the student in getting to the next level of understanding.

We can illustrate this method of refinement by looking at an example of addition and subtraction of positive and negative integers. A teacher may begin by teaching students to order integers and then move to simple concepts of adding positive integers or negative integers only. When the students are ready, the teacher would introduce more complex problems, such as subtracting a positive integer from a negative or adding a positive integer with a negative integer. In the end, the teacher would expect that students could solve all types of integer problems given at random.

That same teacher should also expect that several students might be completely lost. For these students, the teacher may have to reteach using a number line as a scaffold. Seeing how numbers move up and down the number line could help students understand the concept of adding and subtracting integers. Also, seeing that the number line extends from both directions at zero may help a student better understand the concept of negative integers. From there the teacher could go back and teach the discreet skills once again.

For those students still not successful with this alternate approach, the teacher could then meet with them individually to determine where the breakdown was occurring. If the teacher determined that a student was having trouble with addition and subtraction, the teacher might provide manipulatives and teach the concepts using only positive numbers. If the student was proficient with positive integers but getting confused with negative integers, the teacher might assign only negative integer problems until the student was proficient. The teacher would continue to refine his or her approach and provide scaffolds until the desired outcome was reached.

An additional suggestion for refining the approach that a teacher takes involves not only the way the material is delivered to the student, but also the way the student is assessed. By isolating the breakdown in learning through an item analysis of the assessment tool, we may discover that we just need to provide different ways for students to practice the new learning and demonstrate their knowledge. For example, if the data shows that seventh grade students are low in algebra we need to break that information down into more specific and manageable chunks.

First: Identify the Goal

Just saying that students are low in algebra skills does not give us much information. We must therefore break down algebra expectations for the grade level into discreet skills. For a seventh grader, it might be that students need to be able to solve a system of two linear equations in two variables algebraically and be able to interpret the answer graphically. Students might also need to solve a system of two linear inequalities in two variables and to sketch the solution set. Once identifying the discreet skills and learning goals, it will be easier to isolate the difficulty that the student is having.

Second: Isolate the Difficulty

To isolate the difficulty a student is having in learning a specific concept, start by critically looking at student work and asking key questions. For our algebra example, questions might be phrased like this: Are students able to show their understanding of the standards when presented with a computational application but not when it is a conceptual representation? Perhaps they are able to demonstrate the knowledge of the algebraic concept only in a problem-solving situation. As educators have we ensured that our students are given multiple opportunities in various ways to practice the information they are being held accountable for? If we know which type of problem is most difficult, we can then provide targeted instruction and specific practice.

Figure 6.1 shows three questions from a seventh grade algebra assessment where the above learning goal is represented in three very different ways.

It is possible that a student may be able to demonstrate understanding of a concept in one of these formats, yet not all. That is when it is important to know and understand the format of the assessment the student will be given.

Figure 6.1. Test Questions, Seventh Grade Algebra

1. Solve this system of equations:

    $$4x - y = 10$$
    $$2x = 12 - 3y$$

    A. (1, –2)
    B. (3, 2)
    C. No solution
    D. Indefinitely many solutions

2. Graph the following system of inequalities:

    $$2x - y > -3$$
    $$4x + y < 5$$

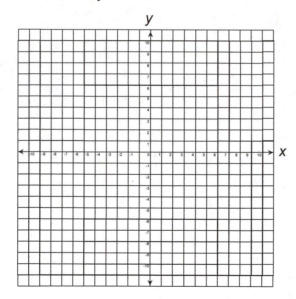

3. The sum of a two-digit number is 9. When the digits are reversed, the number is increased by 9. Find the number.

    A. 63
    B. 45
    C. 27
    D. No solution

Third: Know Your Tests

If we are only providing one type of question for students to show us what they know and are able to do, but this kind of questioning is not aligned to the assessment tools we are using, then our students are being done a disservice. Figure 6.2 graphically illustrates this. In Figure 6.2, we completed an item analysis of a publisher's year-end test and found that a majority of the problems are computational. However, the majority of the questions on the state standardized test, also determined by an item analysis, are conceptual in nature. We also discovered that several more questions are in the form of problem solving. If we only use our publisher's test to give us information regarding our students' level of mastery of algebra, we will be sadly surprised when we receive our state test scores.

Figure 6.2. Comparison of Publisher Year-End Test Questions to State Standardized Test Questions

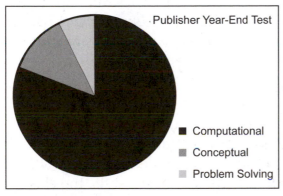
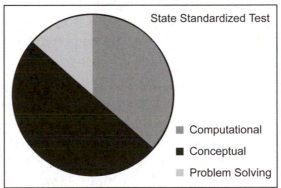

Action Step 3: Know Your Students

Before we can truly make a difference for the students in our classroom, we need to honestly know who they are and what they need. We must personalize the data that we are looking at and change the numbers into names. It is not uncommon for teachers to be told that 20% of their students are below grade-level standards, but what does that mean for the day-to-day planning of instruction. In a class of thirty we know that 20% equates to six students. This gets us closer to being able to develop a plan, but it is not close enough. When we look at the specific six students and assign a name to them, we are then in a place to identify the skills and strategies that require support for these students to meet benchmarks.

Refinement of instruction not only applies to how we approach our teaching, but also to the assignments we are giving our students. Once we know who the students are we can begin to identify what motivates them and provide choice in knowledge demonstration.

How many times have you been given directions to a new location over the phone and wish that someone would just write them down for you? Perhaps you have been given written directions, but really need to see a map? Maybe you need a combination of these strategies to reach your destination without getting lost. Or, maybe, to really feel confident, you will need to actually drive there yourself. This is no different than the way our students reach their final outcomes for learning.

Students, who are given a choice regarding not only how they access new information, but also how they demonstrate their learning, are more likely to be successful at accomplishing any given task. For example, if the learning target is to figure out the area of a polygon, some students may choose to use the algebraic formula to solve the problem. Others may want to use graph paper to draw the shape and count the square units, whereas a different group may opt to use manipulatives, such as cubes, to physically build the shape. No matter what approach is used, all students will be given the opportunity to demonstrate their understanding of the concept being taught based on their individual learning style.

Refinement of choice could also be in how students choose to access or present their information. If the task is to learn about the Holocaust, some students may choose to do a search on the Internet to find information, another may choose to review printed resources from the local library, and yet another may choose to interview a survivor. For their output, those same students may wish to write a research paper or start a blog. Some may do an oral presentation for the class or create a pod cast. And others may choose to create a video or slide presentation. No matter the path or output, the students are held accountable for demonstrating the content. If one approach doesn't yield that result, teachers must again return to the cyclical pattern, beginning with identifying learning objectives. They could then refine their instruction to provide students the ability to choose a different way to provide data that shows evidence of learning.

Be forewarned, however, that although this will solve the issue of determining student understanding, it will not necessarily solve the universal testing dilemma. When asked to perform on a standardized test, students may not always have the luxury of choices or resources available. Therefore, we recommend using choice to master a concept and then practice in different ways. This is true refinement of instruction.

Action Step 4: Monitor As You Go

No matter how much instructional refinement we implement, it will all go to waste unless we are openly and honestly evaluating what we are teaching. As professionals we need to examine the intended versus the implemented curriculum. All the good intentions in the world will not make a difference in student achievement if we do not actually teach with fidelity what we know the students need to learn. Have we actually taught the intended curriculum in enough depth, in the right order, and over enough time? When we take the time to assess student learning can we honestly say that we took our students an inch wide and a mile deep in order to ensure mastery of key concepts or did we only touch the surface of a broad range of topics?

This stage of refinement requires a variety of instructional approaches to meet the needs of all of the students. Collaboration with grade-level and/or subject matter colleagues regarding successes or roadblocks is essential. Evaluation aligned to learning outcomes will help to determine whether it is time to reteach or extend the learning and for which group of students.

Through conferencing and feedback, teachers can communicate to their students how to improve and help them to self-assess their degree of progress toward attaining their own goals. Ongoing formative assessment continues to provide opportunities for success by guiding instructional refinement.

When Refinement Is Not Enough

Although we have outlined a process to promote success and high levels of achievement for all students, we would be remiss if we stopped here. As professionals we understand that not all of our students will respond to the level of differentiation that can be provided in a regular classroom setting. When we look at a response to intervention model, we must acknowledge that some students will need a more intensive approach to intervention than others. These students may be English Learners, special education students, or even students with large gaps in their learning do to irregular attendance or health issues.

Consider, for example, English learners. These students might be extremely capable of identifying the setting of a story, but do not have the vocabulary to articulate or write about it. The teacher could still verify that the student understands the concept by asking the student to point at pictures for their response. This is refinement of instruction. However, if the goal is that the student be able to write a paragraph incorporating the setting, the student may need more English language development instruction before being able to attempt this task. These second-language learners will need specialized instruction to maximize their learning outcomes.

In addition, a small percentage of our students may need special education services to meet their needs. If a student has a learning disability such as an auditory processing delay, the teacher might provide a written copy of the lesson-which is refinement of instruction. However, it might take that student hearing information several times and in smaller more manageable chunks to be able to accurately apply that information. Teachers trained in this type of disability would have specific strategies to help this student learn the given content. This might need to occur in an alternate setting outside of the traditional classroom structure.

Finally, a student might come to a classroom with large gaps in his or her learning. This may be for any number of reasons, such as excessive absences or moving a lot. In this instance, the teacher should not revert back to previous grade-level standards in lieu of teaching the current grade-level concepts. Instead, this student may need tools or scaffolds to support his or her learning. Consider an example of multiplication. If a teacher needs to teach multiple-digit multiplication to her students, but a student never learned his basic facts, the teacher may need to provide a fact chart for the student to reference during the lesson; again, refining instruction. That student also would need more specialized instruction to help fill in for his missing skills. This might occur in a small group or through individualized instruction.

These examples are critical, and not to be ignored. They are the next level of instructional refinement. However, they are also beyond the scope of this book. This book instead helps you to refine your skills so that they may be used to address any specific need of your students or program.

Summary

Are we differentiating our instruction to meet the needs of all of the learners in our classrooms? What intervention and or remediation processes are in place to ensure the success of all of the students? Have we taken the time to get to know our students in such a way that we can motivate them to learn and provide multiple opportunities for their strengths to show? "By thoughtfully using assessment, the teacher can modify content, process, or product" (Tomlinson, 1999, p. 11). To be the most effective, all instruction must be part of a cyclical pattern—a pattern of identifying objectives, collecting data, recording evidence, and refining instruction. This book has taken you through the steps of this cycle.

Many times, teachers are adept at collecting and analyzing data, but don't know what to do with the information, especially if the students are not showing sufficient growth. Therefore, they hit a wall, and the cycle ends. For example, fourth or fifth grade teachers may observe low reading scores but may not be trained to diagnose what part of the early reading process (phonics, phonemic awareness, tracking, etc.) the student is missing.

If learning is truly to be the constant, then we are obligated to restructure our approach to instruction. This is actual refinement of instruction. When a student doesn't understand a concept the first time, it doesn't mean that we should repeat the lesson with *more of the same* types of examples. To provide students multiple opportunities for understanding, you are going to have to find other ways to explain what you are trying to tell them. Likewise, if someone doesn't speak English, it does not make sense to repeat yourself louder and slower; rather, it makes more sense to communicate the same message in a totally new way.

As professionals we must ensure that we are taking all of the necessary steps to increase student achievement whether by actions that are in our immediate control or through a more formalized team approach. This is where vertical teaming is very helpful. In the vertical teaming model, teachers are provided with the time and the structure to meet with colleagues from other grade levels and different areas of expertise whom they are able to ask questions about strategies to teach skills and content beyond their area of focus. They are also able to share their own knowledge, thus expanding their circle of influence and creating a larger capacity to meet the needs of all students.

Conclusion

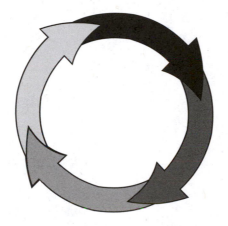

So let's review. We started this journey on a trip to better understand and use formative assessments. More succinctly, we aimed at uncovering ways to actually test less, yet assess more. We demonstrated the importance of being able to identify and define current assessments so that each type can be strategically used. Once the purpose for each is determined and common definitions are established, we can more accurately and clearly look at our own assessment tools.

If educators are ever truly going to successfully move into the twenty-first century, educators will have to leave old testing habits behind. Of course, we aren't suggesting abandoning testing altogether, but the days of the one-room schoolhouse are long gone. Because educators do not have control over all of the required testing for their students, it is all that more critical for educators to be deliberate about what they do have control over. Equally, for those administrators having just read this book, we beseech you to encourage and grant your teachers permission to try this approach.

Remember to begin by writing down every test and looking at the amount of testing we unnecessarily impose upon our students. Then, sort all of those tests by "must-do" and "may-do," identifying those that are nonnegotiable, that is, those over which we have little, if any, power. Undoubtedly, you will face a finite list of predominantly summative tests.

From there, break it down again by sorting your "may-do" tests into formative and summative, keeping only those summative tests that are not addressed through the mandated list. With the remainder of the formative tests, decide if there might be a better way to collect and monitor your students understanding of the subject matter. Go back to the chapters in this book to help you create your own system for assessing without endless testing.

Identify objectives and make every assignment meaningful. If the end result does not provide a picture of student learning, was the time we spent worth spending? Design and refine so that almost every assignment can be used as a form of assessment. Collect data along the way so that you are not forced to give a test that would potentially uncover an unwanted truth that students did not learn the desired outcomes.

To help you better collect this data, have another look at rubrics and scoring guides, goal-tracking sheets, verification logs, evidence collections, and exit slips. Set goals and decide how you will record the evidence of student progress. Experiment with the templates suggested in this book and modify them to best suit the needs of your students. Pitch your traditional grading system and pledge to align your reporting procedures to reflect substantiation of accurate student knowledge and application abilities.

Are we there yet? Perhaps not, but we are certainly on course. Some of us may just be starting the journey, others en route, and some finding themselves in need of a U-turn. No matter where you are, the most important thing is that you have your map and final destination in mind. We hope that this book has provided you with direction and some simple steps toward refining how you approach formative assessments. As you move forward, we recommend keeping this book handy as a guide, for one should never be afraid to stop and ask for directions.

Appendices

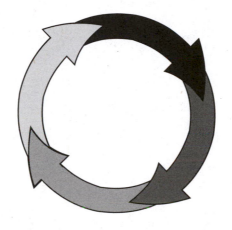

Appendix A: Goal Tracking

Goal:

Name	Date									

Key: 4: Advanced/Independent 3: Proficient/Instructional 2: Basic/Developing 1: Below Basic/Beginning

Appendix B: Goal Tracking

Learning Goal:

Name:		Name:	
Strengths	**Next Steps**	**Strengths**	**Next Steps**

Name:		Name:	
Strengths	**Next Steps**	**Strengths**	**Next Steps**

Name:		Name:	
Strengths	**Next Steps**	**Strengths**	**Next Steps**

Name:		Name:	
Strengths	**Next Steps**	**Strengths**	**Next Steps**

Appendix C: Student Reflection Sheet

Name: _____

Date: _____

Goal:

I can...			

Appendix D: Student Reflection Sheet

Name: _____

Date: _____

Goal:

My work demonstrates...			
	👍	👎	👎
	👍	👎	👎
	👍	👎	👎
	👍	👎	👎
	👍	👎	👎
	👍	👎	👎
	👍	👎	👎
	👍	👎	👎

Appendix E: Exit Slips

Exit Slip

Name: _____ Date: _____

Learning Goal: _____

Demonstration of Understanding:

Exit Slip

Name: _____ Date: _____

Learning Goal: _____

Demonstration of Understanding:

Exit Slip

Name: _____ Date: _____

Learning Goal: _____

Demonstration of Understanding:

Appendix F: Benchmark Tracking

Subject: _____   Student Name: _____   Trimester: _____

Learning Objectives	Benchmark	Date					

Appendix G: Assessment Feedback Tool

Name: _____ Subject: _____ **Student Learning Goals** **Key Standards** **Report Card Descriptors**	Assignment/Assessment										

4: Advanced   3: Proficient   2: Basic   1: Below Basic

References

Ainsworth, L. (2003). *Unwrapping the Standards: A Simple Process to Make Standards Manageable*. Englewood, CO: Advanced Learning Press.

Chappuis, J. (2005, Nov.). Helping students understand assessment. *Educational Leadership, 63*(3), 39–43.

Covey, S. (1989). *7 Habits of Highly Effective People*. New York: Free Press.

DuFour, R., DuFour, R., Eaker, R. (2005). *On Common Ground: The Power of Professional Learning Communities*. Bloomington, IN: Solution Tree.

English, F. (1992). *Deciding What to Teach and Test*. Thousand Oaks, CA: Corwin Press.

Fisher, D., and Frey, N. (2007). *Checking for Understanding: Formative Assessment Techniques for Your Classroom*. Alexandria, VA: ASCD.

Glasser, W. (1998). *The Quality School Teacher*. New York: Harper Collins.

Guskey, T., and Bailey, J. (2001). *Developing Grading and Reporting Systems for Student Learning*. Thousand Oaks, CA: Corwin Press.

Hirsh, S., and Killion, J. (2007). *The Learning Educator*. Oxford, OH: National Staff Development Council.

Leahy, S. (2005, Nov.). Assessment, minute by minute, day by day. *Educational Leadership, 63*(3), 19–24.

Love, N. (2004). *The Data Coach's Guide to Improving Learning for All Students*. Thousand Oaks, CA: Corwin Press.

Marzano, R. (2006). *Classroom Assessment and Grading the Work*. Alexandria, VA: ASCD.

Marzano, R. (2001). *Classroom Instruction That Works: Research-Based Strategies for Increasing Student Achievement*. Alexandria, VA: ASCD.

McTighe, J., and O'Connor, K. (2005, Nov.). Seven practices for effective learning. *Educational Leadership, 63*(3), 10–16.

McTighe, J., and Wiggins, G. (1998). *The Understanding By Design Handbook*. Alexandria, VA: ASCD.

O'Connor, K. (2002). *How to Grade for Learning: Linking Grades to Standards*. Thousand Oaks, CA: Corwin Press.

Reeves, D. (2008). Effective grading. *Educational Leadership, 65*(5), 85–87.

Schmoker, M. (1999). *Results: The Key to Continuous School Improvement*. Alexandria, VA: ASCD.

Stiggins, R., Arter, J., Chappuis, J., and Chappuis, S. (2004). *Classroom Assessment for Learning: Doing it Right—Using it Well*. Portland, OR: Assessment Training Institute.

Tabor, M. *Coaching for Excellence*. Organizational Dynamics Associates, Inc. 23531 Lochlomond, Laguna Niguel, CA 92677. odatabor@aol.com (unpublished).

Tomlinson, C. (1999). *The Differentiated Classroom: Responding to the Needs of All Learners*. Alexandria, VA: ASCD.

Wormeli, R. (2006). *Fair Isn't Always Equal: Assessing & Grading in the Differentiated Classroom*. Portland, ME: Stenhouse Publishers.